BETRAYALS OF THE BODY POLITIC
The Literary Commitments of Nadine Gordimer

ANDREW VOGEL ETTIN

BETRAYALS
OF THE BODY
POLITIC
The Literary
Commitments
of Nadine Gordimer

University Press of Virginia
Charlottesville and London

THE UNIVERSITY PRESS OF VIRGINIA

Copyright © 1992 by the Rector and Visitors of the University of Virginia

First Published 1993

LIBRARY OF CONGRESS CATALOGING-IN-PUBLICATION DATA

Ettin, Andrew V., 1943–
    Betrayals of the body politic : the literary commitments of Nadine
Gordimer / Andrew Vogel Ettin.
        p.   cm.
    Includes bibliographical references and index.
    ISBN 0-8139-1430-2
    1. Gordimer, Nadine—Political and social views.   2. Politics and
literature—South Africa—History—20th century.   3. South Africa in
literature.   I. Title.
PR9369.3.G6Z65   1993
823—dc20   92-27675
                                                                            CIP

PRINTED IN THE UNITED STATES OF AMERICA

FOR MY FAMILY

CONTENTS

ACKNOWLEDGMENTS

I am grateful for an R. J. Reynolds Research Leave from Wake Forest University in the spring of 1989, which allowed me to begin writing this work.

Cathie Brettschneider, humanities editor for the University Press of Virginia, deserves special gratitude for her encouragement and interest during the completion of the manuscript. I also wish to thank the press's readers for their prompt and helpful recommendations.

Among current and former colleagues at Wake Forest who have been particularly supportive, I am especially appreciative of Robert Hedin, as good a poet as a friend, and (once again) Mary K. DeShazer, Dolly A. McPherson, and Lee Potter.

I have also had the good fortune to write with the support of my extended family, whose affection and support I deeply appreciate: my mother, Cecil Ettin; my wife, Carole Stuart; Anna and Emily; and Johanna.

It has been gratifying to conclude this study during the time when the significance of Nadine Gordimer's work was acknowledged through the 1991 Nobel Prize for Literature and to write these final words on the day after a referendum has confirmed South Africa's movement toward full rights of citizenship for all its inhabitants.

March 18, 1992

ABBREVIATIONS

References to the following books by Nadine Gordimer are identified in the body of the text by an abbreviation and page number. The abbreviations correspond to the following editions of the works:

BD   *Burger's Daughter* (New York: Viking, 1979)
CN   *The Conservationist* (New York: Viking, 1975)
GH   *A Guest of Honour* (New York: Viking, 1970)
J   *Jump and Other Stories* (New York: Farrar, Straus and Giroux, 1991)
JP   *July's People* (New York: Viking, 1981)
LBW   *The Late Bourgeois World* (New York: Viking, 1966)
LD   *The Lying Days* (London: Gollancz, 1953)
· MSS   *My Son's Story* (New York: Farrar, Straus and Giroux, 1990)
OL   *Occasion for Loving* (New York: Viking, 1963)
· Sel   *Selected Stories* (Harmondsworth: Penguin, 1983)
SN   *A Sport of Nature* (New York: Alfred A. Knopf, 1987)
SOT   *Something Out There* (Harmondsworth: Penguin, 1985)
WS   *A World of Strangers* (Harmondsworth: Penguin, 1962)

**BETRAYALS
OF THE
BODY POLITIC**
The Literary
Commitments of
Nadine Gordimer

INTRODUCTION

"I'm going to be the one to record, someday, . . . what it was like to live a life determined by the struggle to be free" (*MSS*, 276). These words, be they taken as prognostication or pledge, from the young narrator of Nadine Gordimer's most recent novel express the reason why, for readers outside South Africa, Gordimer's work holds particular fascination. As she certainly comprehends, one of the inescapable consequences of South African politics is that some of this fascination is extra-literary: though she surely ranks among the greatest contemporary fiction writers in English, we also read her for a progressive white's view of "the situation." From the late 1940s onward, beginning with works published in Gordimer's early twenties, through ten novels, more than two hundred short stories, and more than fifty essays on Africa and Africans, on apartheid, on the obligations and rights of the writer, and on the tyranny of censorship, Gordimer has given us an ongoing text to set alongside news reports, editorials, official proclamations, and opposition position papers. To these writings we must also add not only speeches but countless interviews, a fine selection of which appears in *Conversations with Nadine Gordimer*, reflecting more than thirty years of persistent interest in her "amazingly consistent" opinions about South Africa in addition to the usual literary questions.[1] Through her words we have come to know something of the inner experience of South African life for an artist, a reader, a politically engaged intellectual sympathetic to socialist ideals, during a period that has coincided with the rise of the National party and its multitudinous laws for separation and suppression, with the supplanting of colonialism elsewhere in Africa and the more recent dismantling of many structures of apartheid in Gordimer's country, and with the risky revisions of social, political, and

1

economic possibilities necessitated by the disappointments of twentieth century socialism.

Since 1952, when her work began appearing outside of South Africa, Gordimer has come to express the dilemmas of South African life for white readers around the world. She has succeeded Olive Schreiner, William Plomer, and Alan Paton, each of whom played that role for preceding generations, represented a different focus on their country, and articulated a different yet principled response to the main issue of the racism embedded in its custom, attitude, and law. In her own time Gordimer has also overshadowed other notable white South African writers, for instance, André Brink, J. M. Coetzee, and Breyten Breytenbach, as well as outstanding black writers whose cause she has long championed, such as Dennis Brutus, Es'kia Mphahlele, Bessie Head, Alex La Guma, and Peter Abrahams. Gordimer's preeminence arises to some extent from the accident of her social class and race: Like most of her readers both inside and outside her country, Gordimer is white and writes most often (though by no means exclusively) from the viewpoint of middle-class white characters. To some extent, her position also results from the linguistic fact that she writes in English rather than in Afrikaans or one of the non-European African languages and from the formalistic factor that her genre is realistic fiction.

To point out these considerations is not to diminish the stature of her writing; rather, it is to acknowledge, as she herself always does, that such sociocultural considerations count in the reception and accessibility of art. No matter how much one might want to believe in the power of absolute aesthetic merit, the artist works and publishes (when able) within a culture that celebrates some expressive statements more than others, often for reasons having much to do with societal concerns. For example, Gordimer had been rumored a leading candidate for the Nobel Prize for several years before she actually received it, with much speculation centering on the notion that it would seem insensitive if a white South African were the recipient of the first Nobel Prize in literature to be awarded to an African writer. When the Nigerian author Wole Soyinka became the laureate in 1986 and Egypt's Naguib Mahfouz in 1988, many believed that a prize for Gordimer might appropriately follow the recognition of these two African artists, one black and the other Arab; it did, of course, in 1991.

Working as she has generally done within the traditions of realistic fiction, reflective of daily living conditions within a constantly changing political and social context, interested in and aware of those who are themselves agents of change, and just as importantly publishing regularly, Gordimer has become for us the foremost of (to play on the title of her own brief survey of black African writers) the white interpreters. She, in turn, has a number of her own interpreters who have focused principally on the political and ideological dimensions of her work. Understandably, we cannot avoid political and ideological issues; not only do they seem inescapable for anyone writing about a South African author but they are explicitly engaged by Gordimer's creative work. Still, her fiction also deserves to be seen for the art that it is, not because art is greater than life, but because her writings remind us that art and commitment need not be antithetical.

Previous books on Gordimer's writings have concentrated almost exclusively on her novels. This too is understandable. So often linked to historically specific conditions within contemporary Africa (especially South Africa) during the years of their composition, the ten novels published over thirty-seven years (from *The Lying Days* in 1953 to *My Son's Story* in 1990) afford a clear way of tracing the development of the author's thought during the major part of her career as well as her responses to particular events and conditions. These features are likely to be most fully revealed in the larger dramatic space of a novel. Her novels constitute a running commentary on changes in South African society and politics over the past four decades. If, in consequence, the extensive body of extraordinary short stories seems by contrast slighted except by readers, one recognizes the critic's logistical difficulty. Given the richness of the novels and the fascinating correlations they afford between history and the author's chronology, how does one also contend with an even longer career of short-story writing that embraces so many items, with sometimes-complicated publishing chronologies? Yet Gordimer not only began her literary career as a short-story writer but has remained one throughout her life, and her works in this genre have been both memorable in themselves and significant in the unfolding of her literary universe. Therefore, although full treatment of her work in this genre remains beyond the scope of this study, we will pursue relations between the themes and literary strategies of selected stories and the novels.

Gordimer has expressed her own sense of artistic duality, "the two presences within—creative self-absorption and conscionable awareness," stressing too that the writer "must resolve whether these are locked in death-struggle, or are really foetuses in a twinship of fecundity."[2] My goal has been to explore more broadly the process of the artist's "creative self-absorption," without losing sight of her "conscionable awareness." Notwithstanding the importance of Africa in general and South Africa in particular in Gordimer's work, the area constitutes a "content" and context for her writings: "the matter of Africa," it might be called. This book shows how within the space of that African content, but outside it as well, she has explored thematic and literary issues of confidence and betrayal, negotiations of power, tensions of family connections and separations, the urgent compulsions of sexuality, and the narrative strategies of fiction by no means limited to that geopolitical sphere.

For it is Gordimer the artist and the interpreter of lives whose work will continue to hold us, even after that time when South Africa has been (in Yeats's phrase) "changed utterly." Granted, her writings will remain invaluable illuminations of the interior life during the latter half of the twentieth century on a continent in transition and a nation in trauma; her career will also stand as an example of an artist who has managed to work not only *at* but *on* her craft throughout her life while remaining in constant "conversation" about her milieu. Still, even as we read *Sentimental Education* and *A Passage to India* regardless of our curiosity about the political psychology of life in Flaubert's France or Forster's India, readers will turn to Gordimer's writings because of their creative power and human insight. The literary energy derives in great measure from the intensity of political commitment and of conscience, but the one does not substitute for or equate with the other. The best will in the world does not necessarily produce a finely realized story; nor does the well-wrought tale necessarily enlighten its readers by one candlepower about our interlocking relations with one another. Gordimer sensed this from early on in her career; the "writerly" sensibility seems ingrained, as indeed it is likely to be in one who was a writer before she was conscious of her political sensitivity.

The organization of this study thus affords a different perspective on Gordimer's career, sanctioned not only by the appropriateness of the method but also by the writer's own description of her work. The chronological approach followed by other critics affords one vantage point, an important one. When she organized her *Selected Stories*, the author explained in her introduction why she arranged them chronologically:

> I myself enjoy following the development of a writer. Then I found that . . . [t]he chronological order turns out to be an historical one. The change in social attitudes unconsciously reflected in the stories represents both that of the people in my society—that is to say, history—and my apprehension of it. . . . What I am saying is that I see that many of these stories *could not have been written* later or earlier than they were. If I could have juggled them around in the contents list of this collection without that being evident, they would have been false in some way important to me as a writer (*Sel*, 13–14).

By this affirmation of the historical context and sequence as important to the writer's sense of what she is doing, we understand that she expects to be seen and believes it important to be seen against the events of her own time and place.

Simultaneously, but on another track, runs a different sort of critical discourse, in which Gordimer views her career as an attempt "to make out of words a total form for whatever content I seize upon" (*Sel*, 10). Here the language implies that the internal event for the writer is the labor of forming, of constructing a form, with the subject itself a matter of whatever takes one's interest: "There are some stories I have gone on writing, again and again, all my life, not so much because the themes are obsessional but because I found other ways to take hold of them; because I hoped to make the revelation of new perceptions through the different techniques these demanded." The disclaimer "not . . . because the themes are obsessional" virtually denies particular autobiographical significance to the recurrent themes, positing instead that the artist's drive to perfect or revise (that is, see anew) has brought her back to rework situations and issues. And yet, who or what is it that occasions these revisions? Perhaps experience itself, the real or apparent changes that occur in the surrounding world, or the developing insight and distancing of the artist who, stepping back, remarks, "*That* didn't quite get it," or, "Now I see what that was all about." This "revisioning" perspective suggests a movement other than simply the linear movement forward through the progression of volumes—rather, to cite Yeats again, "perns in the gyre." The writer's career also includes the recurrent elements that constitute a stable set of issues to which she is drawn throughout her career, regardless of how time's passage may influence her emphases on them or treatments of them. As Gordimer has also claimed, "we all write one book, but we write it piece-meal and from very different points of view throughout our lives. . . . for a writer, your work is your life and it's a totality."[3] The later chapters of this analysis investigate Gordimer's ongoing exploration of several of those themes.

These make clear her literary commitments—that is, her commitments to literature and her commitments expressed in literature. Gordimer, whose work is engaged with the issues of its time even when its subject is not explicitly political, has revealed a debilitatingly burdened and burdensome body politic to us, through its effects on how people live and love. She has done so, moreover, in ways that truly expose it. By exposing, by *betraying*, she has both uncovered the political body's secrets and undermined its pretensions. To do the former, she seems to believe, necessarily means that one will do the latter.

In scope, thesis, and organization this study differs significantly from the few other books on Gordimer's work. As to scope, it draws on all genres of her published work through 1991, considering numerous short stories, essays, and interviews, to present a fuller view of Gordimer's writing and thought than one obtains through the novels alone.

Previous critics of Gordimer's work have seen her in one of two ways:

as a writer conflicted by the tension between the private lives she wants to explore as an artist and the public sphere that she feels called to address as a citizen of South Africa, or as a political novelist, developing a fictional expression of the abuses of power relationships in South Africa. The first approach was already visible in the first book on her work, by Robert F. Haugh, published in 1974.[4] Haugh's thesis (especially ironic in retrospect) was that Gordimer's talent lay in her short stories, which he saw as tightly focused on private relationships; her increasing attention to the larger realm of public issues had drawn her unfortunately, he believed, into writing novels (five of which she had published by then) evincing difficulties in development and in integrating the political with the personal. That perceived dichotomy of public and private themes was interpreted antithetically in John Cooke's 1985 study, which postulated that breaking free from a maternally dominated environment allowed the author (in her own life) and some of her characters in their fictional lives to progress from a private to a public frame of reference; this progress, Cooke claimed, also led the author to move from a detached, objective, "photographic" vision of her environment to an engaged, subjective, "painterly" interpretation of it.[5]

The second approach, understanding her essentially as a fiction writer fully immersed in her political and historical contexts, was outlined by Michael Wade in his 1978 chronological survey of the development of Gordimer's political ideas, primarily through her novels.[6] More recently, Stephen R. Clingman, a scholar from South Africa, has given us an invaluable reading of Gordimer's development as a historical novelist and thinker. To the reader interested in chronologically tracing nuances as well as the larger shifts in Gordimer's political thought from her earliest writings to the mid-1980s, Clingman's is the one essential guide. It also imparts an extensive familiarity with the details of South African political life, including the complex doctrinal and pragmatic issues arising within the broad range of antiapartheid groups. This book draws on unpublished or generally unavailable material from Nadine Gordimer herself, explored through cogent and literarily acute readings of the first eight novels taken in sequence to trace the development over time of the novelist's political awareness as embodying (in the words of his subtitle) "History from the Inside."[7] Clingman has also edited a selection of Gordimer's essays, under the title of *The Essential Gesture*, with his own introductions helpfully situating each within an historical context.[8] Judie Newman's brief monograph published in 1988 adds significant dimensions to Clingman's readings of the novels as political history by concentrating instead on how inequities of power are expressed through sex, language, and gender relationships in each novel.[9]

Although referring often to the historical contexts in which the works are set and to the issues examined by Newman, I have not tried to replicate the viewpoints of either. This book works in the other direction from Clingman's by showing how Gordimer's perceptions about her own life and about sensual experience, personal interactions, and family relationships (as expressed in her fiction, essays, speeches, and interviews) are reciprocally linked to her political consciousness. I argue that Gordimer has always seen the political as inseparably related to the personal, although her conscious understanding of that relationship has developed profoundly over her career. From the works published in her twenties onward, she has explored in her writings the network of emotional and psychological relationships among characters, but at the same time she has shown that race, class, ethnicity, and gender translate into power within the private and public spheres. Focusing as so many critics do on only one such aspect or one genre to view her work tends to distort or flatten the experience of reading Gordimer, so obscuring one of the most significant features of her writing: her complex awareness of these relationships, embodied as they are in her fiction and articulated in her expository analyses of South African life.

Thus, Gordimer has demonstrated throughout her career that apartheid is not only oppressive to nonwhites but also affects every aspect of people's relations with one another and their concepts of themselves. She has also suggested, through those of her works set outside of South Africa, that apartheid may be grasped as a systematic structure institutionalizing the deceptions and abuses of power and trust to which human beings are given even in their private lives. Apartheid, she reveals, is not an anomaly but a clearly visible manifestation of attitudes and actions common in wider human experience or behavior. Apartheid codifies our oppressive tendencies to separate to segregate, contain, and dominate.

This thesis influences the organization of the book. I would claim that, though her emphases change from work to work and her sophistication as a political thinker as well as an artist has deepened over the years, Gordimer's career should also be explored through the connected concerns and themes recurring throughout her career. Without underestimating the value of tracing changes in Gordimer's political consciousness and commitments through time, I believe her numerous and diverse writings reveal a remarkably coherent body of interests and concerns.

Consequently, instead of working chronologically, I organize my commentary around topics and themes that seem persistent in her discussion of herself as a person and a writer and in her writings themselves. Throughout this work, there are analyses of most of her novels and numerous stories, and I hope that these will claim the reader's interest in their own right. I have not sought to make this book a compilation of individual "readings" of each major work so much as a reading of the one "book" on which she has been working throughout her career.

We start with issues of social self-identity because Gordimer has stressed the degree to which consciousness of one's social identity is an inescapable fact of living in South Africa. In chapter one, while establishing a biographical context, we examine Gordimer's views of herself as a white African, a woman, and a Jew, discussing why she accepts the first as a defining category more readily than the latter two. In so doing, we will also consider her critique of feminism within the South African racial context and her equivocal relationship with her Jewish background as it relates to her personal experience and her views on South African history and society.

Chapter two concentrates on some of her earliest publications. Here we see how she arrives at a consciousness that takes her beyond the restricted cultural and sociopolitical outlook of the mining town in which she grew up. We then probe how she perceives connections between private experience and political context in these early writings.

Chapter three focuses on sensuous experience, which Gordimer identifies as the starting point for her writing interests. This chapter explores how the sensuous continues to figure in her work through her treatment of descriptions and physical details as well as through her careful attention to the meaning of sexual relations for her characters. Relating these to discussions in earlier chapters, we inquire into the connection between physical awareness ("knowing through the body") and political awareness in light of Gordimer's observation that apartheid and other forms of discrimination are built on attitudes toward skin color and hair texture.

The next two chapters analyze Gordimer's treatment of two related forms of deception with which she has also been concerned from early in her career. We turn, that is, from issues of social and physical knowledge to verbal knowledge. Particularly from the vantage point of a writer involved with language and committed to at least attempted honesty about her characters, she perceives that in an oppressive police state our personal as well as public relations with one another will be marked by lies and duplicitous speech (chapter four) and by secrets (chapter five)—sins of commission and omission. We will find that she also shows how such violations of trust occur even in ordinary relations between people outside of this particular political context; however, she does so without undermining the cogency of the political observation or abstracting the specific instance of South Africa into a metaphor or allegory for human life.

We conclude, in chapter six, with her explorations of family tensions and flawed family relationships. This chapter, which also reflects on material presented in the first two chapters, discusses some of her most recent writings, which are stories and novels simultaneously involved with the most personal and the most public conflicts. The family proves to be the microcosm in which we most intensely live out the gratifications and anxieties of sensuality, our lies and deceptions, and our struggles for power built on social as well as personal relationships.

The last chapter thus does not so much introduce a different topic as it draws together issues previously explored in other ways to bring us full circle. In this chapter one can see clearly, as I have suggested from the outset, the persistence of thematic interests from Gordimer's earliest publications to the most recent, the interconnectedness of themes, and the fusion of commitment and comprehension that characterize her work.

The reader already familiar with Gordimer's fiction will enjoy, I hope, exploring more fully the congruity of motifs and concerns as they appear through her writings. I also hope that the curious reader with little knowledge of the author or her writings will be drawn through this study into the wider exploration of her richly nuanced work and find this book not simply a handbook to the interpretation of individual novels or stories but a vade mecum to her "one book," a helpful guide into the complexities and coherence of a career already notable both for its individual and its collective achievements.

CHAPTER ONE

A WHITE WOMAN WRITING
IN SOUTH AFRICA

Nadine Gordimer's career as a writer has coincided with enormous changes in continental African and national South African society and politics, many of which she has recorded through her essays and fiction. Although "human being" and "writer" always seem to be her principal definitions of herself, her awareness of being an African during this period in history should be understood for its deep importance to her and her work. We will begin by trying to grasp in this chapter that conscious sense of African identity, the biographical and literary origins of which will be explored in the next chapter. We will also consider here two other contexts of social identity that have been more problematic for Gordimer, a woman writer of Jewish parentage.

These years during which she has been writing have been crucial in the history of literary and sociopolitical feminism. A female writer whose intense gaze is directed toward the public as well as private realms of life and one who also has depicted many socially conscious, politically involved, and sexually free female characters, Gordimer nonetheless has held herself apart from feminism in her statements on public policy and, to a degree, in her fiction. In contrast to her readiness to identify herself as an African writer, she has particularly rejected classification as a "woman writer." In this chapter we will analyze Gordimer's critique of feminism and her concept of how gender identity has figured in her own development as a writer.

This period has also been momentous in the history of the Jewish people. True, the destruction of European Jewry and the foundation of the modern state of Israel occurred when Gordimer, a child of Jewish immigrants, was already in her twenties. Still, for many people, including many writers, of Jewish or even part-Jewish origins, these events contributed significantly to their self-identity, political consciousness, or moral philosophy. Why Gordimer has not been so affected is a question worth pondering. After all, among the first Jewish communities to be annihilated by the Nazi killing squads and their local collaborators were those in and around Riga, Latvia, where her father's family originated. Furthermore, in acknowledging her Jewish origins, she has remarked on the fascist and Nazi affiliations of many segregationist National party leaders of the 1940s and 1950s as well as on the status of Jews within South African society and politics. While being Jewish in South Africa is not to be compared with being black or even colored, it is no more neutral an identity there than it is most places in the world. Because Gordimer senses so keenly the significance of social identification in shaping one's life, we might expect a more conscious engagement with a Jewish milieu or issues of Jewishness than we do find. Therefore, we will also explore in this chapter Gordimer's connection with Jewishness. In doing so, we will find (as with her response to feminism) that we will learn more about her life and thought, and we will also comprehend more fully what a South African identity means to her.

For Gordimer, claiming an identity as a "white African" is not an oxymoron. While her antiapartheid work as a writer and as a citizen derives from a broad commitment to human rights, it might be fair to say that, for her, apartheid not only denies human rights in general but specifically denies the real essence of South Africa. Her writings register her continuing awareness of multiracialism as a fact—perhaps the one great fact—of that place. Contrast this, for instance, with a text coming out of contemporary San Francisco, Chicago, New York, or London, all multiracial and multiethnic. Although some of that diversity might appear through the mix of accents or the passing of different-hued pedestrians and bit players, it is not unusual at all for people of color to be absent from a white author's novel set in New York City. This is a fact which *should* be unusual, because it is hard to visualize a New York City comprised entirely of Caucasians, and because racial divisions are also facts of living in America. Nor is such separateness only a literary phenomenon.

Questioned in 1987 about analogies between apartheid and the old segregation laws in the United States, Gordimer pointed out significant ways in which apartheid was more radically abusive, yet she observed, "I understand that in this city [New Orleans], the population is roughly 50 per cent black. But I am amazed to see the extent of the division in the few days I've been here. I must confess I've seen more mixing at home."[1] Four years later, the announcement of Gordimer's Nobel Prize coincided with a visit to South Africa by David Dinkins, the African-American mayor of New York City, whose aides took the opportunity to arrange a photo session for publicity purposes. Gordimer, on the other hand, seized the initiative to engage the mayor in a discussion reaching underneath his well-publicized denunciations of South African apartheid and into race relations in America. Her critique repeated the charge she raised in New Orleans. "I find having been coming back and forth between the States now for years that there's more separation now between black and white than there was some years ago, even among the small circle that I move in, of writers, journalists, TV people and people in the arts. We mix much more here under apartheid on that kind of level than they do." Todd S. Burdum, reporting for the *New York Times*, noted that Dinkins, "who seldom reflects openly on such subjects, took up the challenge in a searching spirit that he probably would not have at City Hall," by acknowledging with discomfort the persistent reality of de facto racial segregation in America.[2] That the novelist refused to allow the politician a risk-free publicity opportunity reveals much about her treatment of her own government and her own characters. So too did her courteous yet unflinching opening gambit, like a teacher dealing with a student whom one respects but thinks has not pursued the topic rigorously enough: "I'm going to ask you something hard, and I hope it's not going to upset you." Clearly audible is the implicit declaration that she intends to ask whether it upsets him or not—this rigorous pursuit of evaded knowledge being typical of her public and literary method.

Though a forceful public critic of her own country's policies and of those who approve or tolerate or ineffectually disapprove of them, Gordimer has little patience (as these remarks demonstrate) with foreigners who find South Africa too convenient a target for their moral indignation, not incidentally giving them the opportunity to evade censuring betrayals of principles that occur closer to their own homes. A writer who has sternly denounced censorship in her own country and abroad as well as a political activist drawn to the left, she has nonetheless scrupulously pointed out that although writers in right-wing South Africa have been harassed and imprisoned for their extraliterary activities, in Eastern Europe they have been imprisoned for their writing itself.[3] With a measure of national protectiveness (if not pride) added to her refusal to countenance self-righteousness, she has insisted that injustice and racism are problems not exclusive to South Africa nor of concern only to people of particular ancestry; as she also told the mayor, "I don't think you have to be an interested party, so to speak, to be against racism."

Gordimer takes pride in being a "white African" and attesting that this need not mean being a racist. With ample opportunities to leave, she has avowed an African identity. The place about which she writes is not simply a background or landscape, no matter her obvious affection for that landscape; rather, it and the people who inhabit it are the subject and substance of her art. That place also holds the nation to which she lays at least as much claim as the white supremacists she detests. Accepting the Bennett Award from *Hudson Review* in 1986, she referred to "the country that owns me (for I do not say 'my Africa'—it's the other way round)."[4] The other way round: perhaps the writer's attention comes through here in being precise about how she feels, but so too does the anticolonialist's refusal to *possess* Africa. Not for Gordimer the acquisitive grasp of Robert Frost's, "The land was ours/Before we were the land's." The continuing cost of that notion of manifest destiny, "the gift outright" (in Frost's title) that the privileged can claim by right of birth, is too clearly visible each day in South Africa. Also palpable is the human cost of the commitment. So she responded, firmly, to Mayor Dinkins's disquisition on the preferred status of the term "African-American" by insisting, "But the fact is you're all Americans." Challenging the prerogative of an American of African origins to lay special claim, *beyond* those of human rights, to *possess* Africa—indeed, to displace the voices of Africans who live in Africa but are not black—exposes the oceanic divide. If her riposte to Dinkins implies, make *your* America, it also implies, this is *your* Africa only to the extent that all people are linked in common humanity, as the trade union slogan implies by affirming, "*An Injury to One Is an Injury to All*" (quoted, *MSS*, 117).

Clearly, Gordimer's own relationship, as a writer and citizen, with her South African environment is complex. For much of her career she has been virtually at war with the government's racial and social policies. She has not only revealed their cruelties incisively through her fiction, but in essays and speeches she has expressed her abhorrence candidly and advocated internal and external opposition to those policies. She publicly supported the economic sanctions advocated by the African National Congress (ANC), and upon the unbanning of that organization she immediately joined. Three of her books have been banned in South Africa for periods ranging up to a dozen years; the prohibition of *Burger's Daughter* elicited from her and others a scathing exposé of the country's censorship procedures, as she shrewdly and characteristically used the press against the enemies of the press and the words of the censors themselves to articulate their own ignorance and stupidity.[5] Still, Gordimer has remained devoted to South Africa, a patriot in ways that the right-wing nationalists and Boer separatists could not comprehend.

She has, to be sure, worked free from the more stringent penalties with which other South Africans have been oppressed. Her books have not been banned permanently; she has not been jailed, put under house arrest, or restricted in her public or social activities; nor has she been driven into exile. She has noticed, with some resentment, that some in the literary world at large might like her to have been more persecuted; had she been, she would be a more romantic legend. Despite having spoken frankly even when it was dangerous to do so and made the exposure of apartheid's destructiveness a dominant concern in her fiction, she has disdained the presumption "by self-appointed cultural commissars" that the South African writer is obliged to do so to earn moral credit with the rest of the world. "Can you imagine this kind of self-righteous inquisition being directed against a John Updike for not having made the trauma of America's Vietnam war the theme of his work?" [6] Instead, she has insisted that the artist's moral obligations are to art—this from a writer whose essays constitute a powerful attack on the racial and racially influenced socioeconomic structure of her country.

Still, Gordimer seems to distinguish between the artist's responsibilities and the citizen's obligations, and in this regard she is perhaps not fully immune from the self-righteousness that is so difficult to separate from passionate commitment. For example, during a session devoted to Arab-Israeli issues at a writers' conference in Budapest, she staked claim to her Jewish ancestry and berated Israeli writers for not following the examples of protest set by antiapartheid South African authors to "lay their lives on the line." This stance provoked indignant public responses from the Israelis, all of whom were active in their country's peace movement and found some bitter irony in the fact that the meeting had been boycotted by the invited Arab writers. In private, according to a news account, some wondered rhetorically what life-threatening actions she had taken against her government.[7] This indirectly recalls that, her candor notwithstanding, Gordimer has not engaged in those extraliterary activities that got other people (including writers like Dennis Brutus and Breyten Breytenbach) imprisoned. This too she has acknowledged.

•   On the one hand sneered at as "the blacks' darling" by rightist whites who resent the acceptance given her (personally and artistically) by black artists, she has been attacked on the other by some black separatists resentful of a white author depicting blacks whose lives she cannot share completely.[8] Because she cannot become a black writer, she has insisted that there are ways in which blacks and whites do know one another and therefore deserve the right to write out of that knowledge, while she has also noted that there are indeed ways in which she as a white South African cannot know the lives of black compatriots, this being one of the human costs of apartheid. The societal priorities and aesthetic concerns of black artists and white artists will likely be different in such a land. She has expressed how South African realities shape the limitations and possibilities.

> There are certain experiences of white life that it's very unlikely that any
> black writer would know enough of to write convincingly and the same

applies, only more so, to white writers. But that doesn't mean that I believe that white writers can't create black characters; and that black writers
can't do the same with whites. . . . Although the law has kept us, in some
ways very successfully, apart, there's an enormous area of life where, for
350 years, one way or another—on farms and in town, we have been rub-
bing up against each other in a vast area where our consciousness is inter-
mingled.[9]

I challenge my challenger to deny that there are things we know about
each other than are never spoken, but are there to be written—and received with the amazement and consternation, on both sides, of having
been found out. Within those areas of experience, limited but intensely
revealing, there is every reason why white should create black and black
white characters.[10]

Gordimer thus asserts that both experience and art cross the racial boundaries drawn by social custom and, more brutally, by law. She will also claim
that great art must strive to transcend such boundaries, through the "conscionable awareness" of the social individual who means to see, joined with
the "creative self-absorption" of the artist who will understand and reveal
that understanding through language.[11]

She recognizes, especially because she is a writer, that social circumstances (including access to books) can explain what may appear to be fundamental differences among people of different races. "The business of
relating the social conditions I saw about me to law or to any moral questions came to me from outside, from reading."[12] Perhaps Gordimer's com-
mitedness as a writer can be attributed to her consciousness of the role that
reading had in her own moral development: "Would I ever even be a writer
if I couldn't have gone and used the public library? But no black child could
use that public library."[13] It is that understanding that leads her to stress
the importance of changing "the structure of culture" in a free South Africa
of the future, "where the bookstores are, where the libraries are, [now] in
the white areas only."[14] Her awareness of the social and political conditions
within which culture dwells appears also in her analysis of the government-
owned South African television, on which she has not yet appeared, not
because she has been boycotted but because she has boycotted it. "I banned
myself," she has said, from "the most effective tool for the propagation of
[the government's] ideas." Analyzing the strategy for co-optation, she has
noted that allowing her works to be shown on television or appearing there
in even a purely literary discussion allows the authorities to use this as
evidence of freedom in the country. Notably, she also sees these decisions
not simply as personal matters of conscience but as issues to be decided in
concert with other writers and the leadership of the political organization
she has long supported, the African National Congress.[15]

It is surely telling that the Gordimer's writings are far more fully integrated than is the society of which she writes. Not that she falsifies or writes as if actual barriers did not exist; the fact of separateness is part of her work's reality and realism, but she makes the effort to compensate for the fact by the conscious acknowledgment of "black" or "colored" or "Asian" presences in her work (to use—as circumstances make unavoidable—the terminology of white governmental racialism). Such characters are infrequently central in the novels, although they are more often so in individual stories. Even more rarely does Gordimer use a character from one of these South African legal categories for her narrator or for a narrative perspective. This itself attests to her belief that in a racialist society, there will be limits to one's ability to understand someone of another grouping as if one could be inside that person and think through that mind simply as the mind of another human being, "like yourself" (as Leviticus enjoins us to think about our neighbor). A significant exception is *My Son's Story*, set during the 1980s, when most legal restrictions of "colored" peoples had been rescinded or could be ignored, even if briefly. Choosing a "colored" first-person narrator seems at once to engage the reader's understanding for such a viewpoint and betoken its accessibility, not solely on a private but political level as well.

While "white African" and "African writer" are titles Gordimer accepts easily, though with no facile assumptions regarding their meanings for her life and work, the category of "woman writer" seems more problematic for her. (By way of analogy, one might consider the more extreme example of Cynthia Ozick, who welcomes inclusion of her work in anthologies of Jewish writers and identifies herself as a feminist but who has characterized the classification "woman writer" as artistically irrelevant to real art.)[16] Gordimer's political convictions and treatment of female characters in her works suggest a keen understanding and heightened awareness of the special circumstances of women's lives as well as a remarkable grasp of the appraising, judgmental, emotion-laden ways in which men talk and think about women, in particular and in general. One of the notable aspects of her art is her affecting creations of numerous independent, politically engaged, and sexually (like all of her characters, heterosexually) energetic women. Judie Newman has demonstrated how verbal and narrative details in the novels bespeak connections between gender and power. The strong commitments of Gordimer's own public life, the self-reliant courage shown by many of her female characters, and the importance of community and connectedness in her writings lead many female readers to expect from her both understanding of feminism and affiliation with it. Certainly it is notable that many feminist readers are surprised to find that in her expository works Gordimer is not more explicitly feminist than she is and that she actually eschews a commitment to feminism.[17] Even in her essays (to illustrate this with a stylistic detail) she has adhered until quite recently to the convention by which every theoretical individual, even "the artist," is "he." Is it enough to say this was the habit of long usage, when the writer herself cast off other habits of thinking, both social and literary? Perhaps it is more accurate to say that she, like many female (as well as some male) Africans, sees feminism as right in principle but dangerously distracting from the battle against apartheid in practice. A reviewer who lamented the absence of feminism in the essays urged, "We must return to her fiction for women revolutionaries and for revolutions that turn on the role of women."[18] As we shall see in later chapters, even this assessment requires careful delineation.

Nonetheless, "women revolutionaries," or at least women actively and riskily working against governmental oppression of the African majority, abound in Gordimer's writing from the early works to the present and afford many varieties of resistance or activism, even if one surveys only the novels. Helen Shaw, the somewhat autobiographical narrator of her first novel, *The Lying Days* (1953), runs directly contrary to familial and social patterns in befriending and unsuccessfully trying to offer living space for a black woman student and subsequently is changed in her racial consciousness by the repressive apartheid laws passed after 1948. In the next book, the most committed white activist, the one character who manifests a moral political conscience, is an Afrikaner woman, Anna Louw. The jaded but unsettled female narrator of *The Late Bourgeois World* (1966) is moved near the end of the book to enter into commitment and the process of history in her own small but dangerous way, as she contemplates making a bank account accessible to the banned Pan-Africanist Congress, an offense punishable by a lengthy jail sentence. *Burger's Daughter* (1979) affords so diverse a panoply of female political activism that it deserves to be studied by itself from just that perspective, while *A Sport of Nature* (1987) offers through the central character of Hillela a larger-than-life romance figure of a woman equally at ease in the bedroom and on the battlefield, crucially involved with the politics of a changing Africa. In *My Son's Story*, published in 1990, the sexual and intellectual lover, Hannah, the domestic and quietly maternal wife, Aila, and the sociable and highspirited daughter, Baby, all prove to be committed antiapartheid activists, the last two emerging surprisingly involved with underground activity more dangerously and violently subversive than anything undertaken by the well-known political activist who is husband and father to them. Expressed through them (as it was through Hillela) is a wholeness of commitment contrasting with the man's more analytic appraisal of "positions," tactics, and strategy.

There is no romanticizing of women in politics in this body of work, however; for the list could also include such flawed figures as Ann in *Oc-*

casion for Loving (1963), who tries to spurn the "color barrier" by taking a black lover, only to leave him abandoned to pain and resentment when she proves that she has absorbed the racism of the society to which she feels tied; Antonia, the outspoken liberal in *The Conservationist* (1974), whose actions are fraught with contradictions and failures of nerve and integrity; and Maureen in *July's People* (1981), another white liberal whose convictions are tested and shaken by the challenge of living up to them under duress.

In a review she wrote of a biography of Olive Schreiner, Gordimer makes explicit her priorities and her reasons for those priorities.

> Feminism was [Schreiner's] strongest motivation. Yet the fact is that in South Africa, now as then, feminism is regarded by people whose thinking on race, class and colour Schreiner anticipated, as a question of no relevance to the actual problem of the country—which is to free the black majority from white minority rule. . . . The women issue withers in comparison with the issue of the voteless, powerless state of South African blacks, irrespective of sex. It was as bizarre then . . . as now . . . to regard a campaign for women's rights—black or white—as relevant to the South African situation. Schreiner seems not to have seen that her wronged sense of self, as a woman, that her liberation, was a secondary matter within her historical situation.[19]

In this passage one can recognize a complaint about feminism sometimes made elsewhere as well, particularly by women of color, whose viewpoint Gordimer comprehends. We can also recognize the limits of Gordimer's own view of feminism. It does not seem to take in the perspective that sees feminism as a crucial instrument for dismantling traditional structures of power at all levels, including the global, for instance; nor does it admit the relevance of feminism to comprehending the especially brutal impact of apartheid on black South African women, especially mothers. These are concepts of feminism Gordimer would presumably support, but they are not part of her sense of feminism. Indeed, as we will see, she is convinced from experience that feminism by itself cannot transcend the racial divisions in a racially separate culture.

Although a strong emphasis on the fundamental political impact of feminist thinking is relatively recent, it was most notably anticipated by Virginia Woolf's *Three Guineas*. That book's perceptive analysis of connections between feminism and socioeconomic class issues, as well as its exposure of the complex root system of patriarchal power throughout social institutions, might have stimulated the development of Gordimer's grasp of relationships between feminism and class politics. This in turn might have emphasized the real political depth of a book like *Mrs. Dalloway,* seemingly a foremother of some of Gordimer's fiction in its interplay of multiple voices and revealing juxtapositions of public experiences and private emotions. However, the revival of general interest in Woolf occured after Gordimer's own career as novelist and essayist was already well established; it is worth recalling that she was seventeen at the time of Woolf's death, and she came into her own as an artist during a period of reaction against Woolf and Bloomsbury. Although Gordimer has spoken and written admiringly of the English novelist—"the complexity of her human relationships, the economy with which she managed to portray them . . . staggering"—it has always been in terms associating her with "that transparent envelope that she'd find for herself," the achievement of having "made sense of one small area." Conscious of literary influences on her own writing, Gordimer recognized and obviously held at a distance Woolf's "very dangerous" (because so easily imitated) prose stylistics.[20] On the larger scale Gordimer identifies Woolf with the evolution of the *nouveau roman:* Writers "became fixed on Virginia Woolf's mark on the wall—and as an end, not a beginning," and in so doing, "went as far as it is possible to go from any societal demand."[21] True, she knows the difference between Woolf's beginning and the other writers' endings, and she does admire in Woolf something especially valuable to Gordimer, the sense of place.[22] But the terms of her comments on her great predecessor suggest that she overlooks Woolf's socioeconomic consciousness, an aspect of that writer's work particularly important to contemporary literary and social feminism. Her judgments of Woolf indicate, therefore, Gordimer's predominant sense of feminism's limitations.

Let us situate Gordimer's view of feminism in context. One issue, of course, is the matter of what and when one knows about feminism, which after all does not advance an unchanging or single doctrine. Ozick, to cite her again, as a female writer born only five years after Gordimer, has argued that her generation's notion of feminism—and one's own generation, of course, always has the correct definitions—demands an indifference to gender that makes a term like "woman writer" as antifeminist as "lady doctor" or "poetess," or as dismissive. Gordimer, however, thinks "there *is* such a thing as 'ladies' writing,' for instance, feminine writing; there are 'authoresses' and 'poetesses.'"[23]

Gordimer often treats feminism as an expression of personal and privileged complaint, elitist rather than populist, a movement arising from the particular bourgeois compulsions of a middle-class white intellectual refusing to face up to and militate against her true position of power. Quoting again from her denunciation of Schreiner: "Ironically, here at least she shared the most persistent characteristic of her fellow colonials (discounting the priorities of the real entities around her) while believing she was protesting against racism."[24] The racial situation is "real," and her feminism a sort of surrogate protest through which she could object to her own grievances while acting on behalf of black African women *as women* rather than as Africans. Notice too how the phrase "within her historical situation" implies that oppression against women is more personally than historically significant. Ironically, this criticism, from the opposite direction, actually mirrors Woolf's objection in *A Room of One's Own* to Charlotte Brontë for writing conscious of her personal grievances ("her wronged sense of self," in Gordimer's phrase). Whereas Woolf wanted the pure incandescent filament of artistic consciousness, Gordimer expects understanding of historical conditions.

An even more pressing consideration is Gordimer's pragmatic appraisal of how difficult it is to mobilize effectively against the emergencies of black life in South Africa. Concentrating on anything else does seem distracting, dangerous, and potentially divisive (though there is no inherent reason why feminism should be divisive). Characteristically, she herself locates her reaction to feminism precisely in terms of place and time: It "doesn't seem irrelevant to me in other places in the world, but it does seem at the present time to be a kind of luxury in South Africa. Every black woman has more in common with a black man than she has with her white sisters."[25] In the review article on Schreiner, Gordimer judges the earlier writer's feminism by means of a revealingly condescending statement that seems to denigrate it precisely because it confronts a situation not defined by place and time: "I suppose one must allow that she had a right to concern herself with a generic, universal predicament: that of the female sex."[26] The "generic, universal predicament," in other words, ought to have less claim on one's attention than more particular urgent grievances against which one could apply some effective leverage. In a rare, apocalyptic vision of spiritual liberty breaking forth to purify the world (in the 1984 essay "The Essential Gesture"), Gordimer does imagine that liberation will "cleanse the statute books of their pornography of racist and sexist laws," with this atypical yoking of the two forms of oppression as equal presumably legitimated precisely because the passage expresses a prophetic concept of justice. It is notable that her most sympathetic specific espousal of feminism emerges from a particular economic observation that surely connects with her own early experiences as an impoverished young writer and divorced mother raising a small child herself. "As for my attitude toward feminism . . . I always have become indignant over the fact that women in professions don't have the same working conditions or salaries as men. . . . As soon as a woman is married, if she's a schoolteacher, for example, she's paid less because she's regarded as a poor risk: she's probably going to have a baby and interrupt her career. And if she comes back to teaching when she's older, she is still paid on a lower grade because she is married. This I think is disgusting."[27] Yet Gordimer does not allow this to stand as a purely gender-related issue: "I see it as part of the whole question of human rights and disaffected groups in various societies."

So we see another factor influencing Gordimer's attitude toward feminism. A white woman committed to the liberation of her black compatriots, she senses circumspectly that Schreiner's "wronged sense of self, as a woman" has no place here. Sympathy for feminist programs and goals means that Schreiner directs attention and sympathy toward her own situation as a woman who is white and middle class and consequently away from others who require it "within her historical situation." That sense of self, that consciousness of self, suggests selfishness, which entails turning away from others, embracing a conception of one's own specialness—the trappings of bourgeois privilege, separateness, autonomy. It may also be a way of casting off onto others the responsibility for one's own failings: At times, Gordimer maintains, women are culpable for their own oppression. "I see all around me women who are gifted and intelligent who *do* have these struggles and who indeed *infuriate* me by allowing themselves to be used by men. It's the mental abuse that I think of, really, women who give up their development as human beings because they're willing to subordinate this to some man."[28] By contrast, writing about her own history growing up as a female intellectual, Gordimer has written that "my femininity has never constituted any special kind of solitude, for me."[29] Her use of the equivocal "femininity" is revealingly appropriate here, because she does not mean simply "being a woman." As she continues, "My only genuine and innocent connection with the social life of the town . . . was through my femaleness. As an adolescent, at least I felt and followed sexual attraction in common with others; that was a form of communion I could share. Rapunzel's hair is the right metaphor for this femininity: by means of it, I was able to let myself out and live in the body, with others, as well as—alone—in the mind." Which is to say that for Gordimer, "femininity" was access to the social world. It was the means by which she found and related to others. Recalling her parents' opposition to sending her, two or three years late, to the university, she writes: "It was suggested that (as distinct from the honourable quest for a husband) the real reason why I wanted to go was to look for men. It seems to me now that this would have been as good a reason as any. My one preoccupation outside the world of ideas was men, and I should have been prepared to claim my right to the one as valid as the other."[30] The somewhat equivocal mood of the verb *should* contains the imperative. (Frank acknowledgment that the sexual may easily accompany the intellectual also allowed her to recognize, without specifically naming it as sexist, the desire of many literary journal editors to meet an author "when the contributor is known to be a young girl."[31]) That this was not a passing youthful phase but a social perception she still finds valid is attested to by *A Sport of Nature*, where precisely through sexuality Hillela frees herself from the limits and restrictions of her class and race. So Gordimer has indicated that sexuality and femininity were not restricting and oppressive but liberating to her. "For me": She is also candid in saying, even as she professes the familiar disclaimer, "I really haven't suffered at all from being a woman," that "I would consider it an arrogance to state my own experience as true for all women."[32]

She also has no qualms about accepting sexual impulses—the ones she writes of are heterosexual—as both powerful and acceptable motives for action. Perhaps we can sense through this the outlook of someone assured of her sexual attractiveness; this is also someone keen to recognize the powerful pull of sexuality in human motivation. "Sex and politics . . . politics and sex—I don't know which comes first—have been *the* greatest influences on people's lives." For Gordimer, the two are not polar but complementary. She continues, "Having the revolutionary temperament, the daring, usually goes along with very sexually attractive personalities, strong sexuality in both men and women."[33] The persistence of that connection in Gordimer's thinking is borne out in both *A Sport of Nature* and *My Son's Story*, where it is a major motif. As the narrator writes of the father's lover in the latter book, "Hannah's emotions were those of the world of commitment he and she shared. . . . In her—needing Hannah—sexual happiness and political commitment were one." (*MSS*, 125).

Still, she also claims, more confidently and absolutely than Woolf ventured in *A Room of One's Own*, that "when it comes to their essential faculty as writers, all writers are androgynous."[34] The matter-of-factness with which Gordimer makes this statement about a controversial and speculative idea may suggest the desire simply to put the issue beyond discussion. If so, the reason may be a generational distrust of the "woman writer" compartmentalization; it may also be a covert acknowledgement that the writers she herself most often cites or looks to as kindred spirits seem to be men (Turgenev, Kafka, Lawrence, Sartre, Achebe, Kundera, Milosz, Breytenbach, Beckett) who have been at odds with their society or government; in her Nobel Prize speech she specifically quoted or praised more than thirty writers, past and present, from Africa, Europe, and South America (but not North America), all of them male.[35] Two female writers whom she cited earlier as influential on her work, Pauline Smith and Katherine Mansfield, she acknowledged pointedly for their use of "'colonial' background."[36] Such a designation seems to mark them as local-colorists, defined and delineated by involvement with a colonial culture, marginal in their literary essences. While the reference to Mansfield underscores the degree to which Gordimer's work also fits into the tradition of fiction of manners and social relations, that is indeed the element in her work that she has consciously written against: "I got to hate that word about my work—'sensitive.' I was constantly being compared to Katherine Mansfield."[37] In the same context Gordimer also criticizes, with obvious discomfort, another woman writer, "the greatest American short-story writer ever, Eudora Welty." When one recalls who might be included among the competition, her tribute seems particularly grand; yet a demurral accompanies this, and although Gordimer's remarks about Welty make no reference of any sort to gender but rather to place and circumstance, they recall traditional assessments of women writers' limitations: "She might have turned these incredible gifts of hers more outward—she might have written more, she might have tackled wider subjects." It was of course the "colonial" matter that made the significant connection with Mansfield, and the Southern American environment (with racial patterns evocative of South Africa) that partly accounted for Welty's attractiveness; still, Gordimer feels the scale constricting. Given her perspective as reflected in the remarks regarding Mansfield and Welty, it is not surprising that she praises contemporary Latin American writers more enthusiastically. The ones she cites, albeit in serendipitous recall during an interview, are all male; Borges, García Marquez, Carpentier, Fuentes, Vargas Llosa, Puig—"these just roll off my tongue quickly." Interestingly, she admires their work even though "they all write about the same thing. . . . The themes are as obsessive as the African ones."[38] This limitation clearly is less keenly objectionable than Welty's smaller output and narrower subjects.

Because Gordimer defines herself so strongly as a writer of fiction, this list of writers she admires is tantamount to identifying the most important and deepest part of her nature as androgynous, suggesting another reason why feminism seems not only politically but also personally peripheral to her. The "woman writer," she has said, "is somebody who is setting out to make a point about being a writer," whereas "the special quality a writer has that is not defined by sex" is "the ability to intuit other people's states of mind."[39] The term *androgynous* when used favorably by Gordimer, however, seems really to mean *not gender-limited.* "Henry James could have been a woman. E. M. Forster could have been. George Eliot [whose *Middlemarch* she has cited as influential on her] could have been a man."[40] A writer who crosses over the racial distinctions of her country and her experiential outlook, Gordimer even more frequently crosses over gender distinctions in her own fiction, not only through the ungendered third-person narrator but also through explicitly male narrators such as Toby in *A World of Strangers* and Will in *My Son's Story.* Praising the "apparently fantastical and uncommitted" Michel Tournier, Gordimer commends his view of "the restoration of wholeness (the totality which revolutionary art seeks to create for alienated man) in a form of Being that both sexes experience as one—something closer to a classless society than to a sexually hermaphroditic curiosity."[41] In this way she suggests the value of eliminating class distinctions (because she deplores classism along with racism and sexism) while suggesting that the androgynous vision may transform sexuality into a more generous eroticism.

It is also surely true that Gordimer realizes from South African experience that recognizing one's own oppression, whether as a woman or as anything else, does not lead necessarily toward empathy with other intensely oppressed peoples in one's own country. We see this not only in her response toward Schreiner but more dramatically in her appraisal of the South African novelist Sarah Gertrude Millin, "a remarkable woman, . . . at her best, a remarkably good writer," and yet, "a monster."[42]

Millin is an even more appropriate foil for Gordimer than is Schreiner. Like Gordimer herself, Millin wrote essays on political and social events of her era (from the 1920s into the early 1950s) but in addition to being a "brilliant" intellectual was primarily a novelist of some stylistic individuality and power and, again like Gordimer, Jewish. (Millin, however, continued to identify herself strongly as such; Gordimer, raised assimilated into a secular, vaguely Protestant social environment and schooled first at the Convent of Our Lady of Mercy, acknowledges the Jewish background of her parents but otherwise, for reasons we will explore below, has been personally indifferent to religion and ethnicity). She and Millin are also, of course, if not explicitly feminists and not "women writers," nonetheless South African writers who happen to be women.

Gordimer's particular horror at the "monster" Millin derives from the latter's singular performance "as a passionate defender of apartheid, and a tragi-comic pariah among her peers in South Africa and abroad." She lacked Schreiner's occasional feminist acknowledgments of solidarity with black African women and pronouncements about the positive moral value of elevating the position of South African blacks. Though Millin spoke vigorously against European fascism and denounced Nazi persecution of the Jews, she became a supporter of the Nazi sympathizer and later South African president Jan Vorster in addition to becoming an essayist and novelist with "a pathological prejudice against blacks." For reasons Gordimer suggests (discussed below, in chapter three), Millin does not draw the sort of connection the adolescent Gordimer was able to make when she read of Chicago meat packers in Upton Sinclair's The Jungle ("I can still see that particular edition on the shelf there.") and "began to think about these mine workers that I saw and was taught as a child to be afraid of."[43] Millin's situation raises "many plaguey questions about the relation of creativity to morality," and surely these are not the only kinds of questions raised for Gordimer here.

The questions are as important as the judgments, because they lead to the conclusion that moral awarenesses are not interchangeable. Somehow the creative writer is trapped within the most elementary and thoughtless bigotry of her culture; somehow the opponent of fascism lauds it when it becomes accomplice to her own prejudices; somehow the Jew who denounces anti-Semitism can believe that another form of racism is not merely endurable but right, just as Schreiner, the earlier feminist advocate, could devote much of her writing career to denouncing oppression against women while slighting and in some ways even excusing the subjugation of all black people. With such examples before her of the failure to connect, it is easy to see why Gordimer wishes to reject the implication that "woman-as-intellectual" carries any particular valence.[44] Further, we shall see in the next chapter that Gordimer herself was subject to a striking instance of matriarchal power that would argue against any idealizing of maternal love or female sensibility.

Nor is this a problem of the past. Indeed, Gordimer has specifically criticized the presumption that women's experiences as women transcend their differences, at least in her country.

> We [black women and white women] may share the same convictions, but after we've finished talking about it in sisterly fashion, I remain the privileged writer and she goes back home to where her children are being attacked.
>
> Whenever something terrible happens to young people, . . . to children in South Africa, you get well-meaning white women saying, "We are all mothers. This is something we have, no matter what color we are, that men cannot have because we bear our children." But these organizations, which call themselves Women for Peace or whatever, they always break up because of what has happened to the black women's children. White women's children are going to school every day, working peacefully, and the black women's children are taking on the burden of political responsibility, boycotting school, having tear gas thrown into their classrooms.[45]

In a story dating from the same period as those comments, the late 1980s, Gordimer depicts a white activist asking her school-age black visitors, members of the Youth Congress, about their activities, as she might ask the children of relatives or friends; but from their replies about their political involvements and months of detention in jail, she must recall the political knowledge she possesses but had not yet applied to people with whom she has real experience, the knowledge that, "youngsters their age have not been at school for several years, they are the children growing into young men and women for whom school is a battleground, a place of boycotts and demonstrations. . . . She should have known, she should have known, it's a common enough answer from youths like them, their colour. They're not going to be saying they've been selected for the 1st Eleven at cricket or that they're off on a student tour to Europe in the school holidays" (J, 95–96).

A fuller literary representation of how this state of affairs separates black and white occurs in *Burger's Daughter*, where Flora, veteran of years of activism, invites Rosa to an interracial women's liberation meeting that the older woman hopes will stimulate another sort of liberation. The phrasing recalls Gordimer's own language in interviews, from Rosa thinking that "the rights of women as our kind . . . see these: the oppression of black women primarily by race and only secondarily by sex discrimination," to Flora recalling that "the women's movement in the ANC was a force" and hoping to get her well-meaning suburbanites "to tackle human rights as *women* . . . together. . . . I think it's possible to tap new resources, maybe" (BD, 199, 201). But the search for common issues breaks down as one white woman (who could be an agent provocateur) berates another for her naive racial insensitivity, and as the black women withdraw into their own languages for private conversation or quietly slip out of a scene growing dangerous, another white arises to object ludicrously, "We don't need to bring politics into the fellowship of women" (BD, 203). Despite Flora's embarrassingly earnest reminders about "the common possession of vaginas, wombs and breasts, the bearing of children and awful compulsive love of them," this meeting never focuses on the ones whose presence alone is eloquent, "the silent old blacks still dressed like respectable servants on a day off," mute reminders of the stubborn imperatives of class, the real differences in possibilities and hopes (BD, 204).

In the story "Keeping Fit," it will be just such a woman—"the strict face formed by respectability, a black woman churchgoer's face" (J, 234)—who gives haven to a white jogger when he literally runs into a murderous band of black youths pursuing another black, a scene from the internecine battles of the late 1980s. The woman's exquisite balance of curt hospitality, candor, and aloofness in the squalid two-room shanty where she dwells with the six other members of her family, the place into which she has pushed him out of danger, leaves him sensing her double message: You have been reckless in coming near this squatter's camp; you are so presumptuous that you think you have no limits. There is also her more explicit message, that "tomorrow it can be *him*"—her son; they could "take my son and kill him" (J, 235). That son, she explains, is "in the Youth—the street committee," and he too lives here. The jogger who has feared for his life will return to his suburban comfort, while his rescuer remains amid the terror from which he has run.

Still, it is no surprise that his rescuer is female, whether motivated (so he wonders) by a churchgoer's Christian charity or by a woman's nurturance. As Flora's reference to the women's ANC branch implies, Gordimer is also aware that women, especially in South Africa, have in fact taken on special roles. Asked in an interview to discuss the important role of the Black Sash, a South African women's organization that has worked against forced resettlements of black people, Gordimer described the group's origins and endeavors, its progress, "from being nice liberal ladies who were sorry to see blacks ill-treated [to becoming] really tough, politically minded people," and she continued, "I would like to add one other thing. Why women? Why should it be a women's organization? Where are the husbands of these women? I think it stems from something I realized long ago as a child. When I was a child, such culture as there was really belonged to women. It was the frontier mentality. The men were out earning a living, and if a pianist came and gave a concert, then your mother took you, and she usually took the girls in the family. Culture was a thing for women, and so was liberalism; so was social concern." [46] This analysis suggests that a process of socialization within a particular culture and class, rather than some essentialist female response to issues of home and the arts and family security, accounts for this phenomenon. It also indicates that Gordimer's gender awareness, her feminism, is actually just one facet of her interest in the implications of social place: As she has said about the skill of writing dialogue, what matters is hearing "how people express themselves in different situations and different social and economic classes."

Her distinction between "nice liberal ladies" and "really tough, politically minded people" embodies the distinction between Gordimer and her own mother, whom she also described as "much more conscious of political problems" than her father.

> She was conscious of the fact there was a great mass of people who were very—what she would have called—underprivileged. She worked all her life for the "charitable uplift" of blacks. . . . And the moral lesson was that you were kind and you gave things to people who had less than you had . . . but I don't think my mother ever carried it to its political conclusion; that it was really no good, in the end, handing out clothes or running crèches [nurseries] while the law remained the same. . . . She did have the feeling that these were people like herself, but she accepted the law. [47]

The difference is the level of political awareness. To rephrase that statement in specifically and appropriately feminist terms, the difference between them resides in the readiness to extend from the personal ("if anybody spoke to a black person in a nasty way she would immediately get angry; and I remember her saying many times, 'They ought to remember that they are also human'") to the political ("it was really no good . . . while the law remained the same").

"The men were out earning a living." Political convictions notwithstanding, Gordimer is conscious that social conditions affect people's responses to the political and moral issues of their society. "I have to remind myself often," she says, of her father's upbringing when judging him. That includes remembering that he arrived in South Africa a refugee from anti-Semitism and shtetl poverty "at the age of 13, poor, without knowing any English," to stay with a relative and knowing that such an experience "limits" some people "to cling desperately to any security that they find" and to withhold sympathy from others because they themselves received none. Her mother, by contrast, had immigrated as a child "from a much more comfortable and secure background. There was no hardship at all for her: she went to school here and had no problem of acculturation. English was her tongue and there it was. . . ."[48] So the general observation that "culture was a thing for women" took shape in her own home, where culture extended to the depth of language itself, and it developed not purely as a gender issue for the young Nadine Gordimer but as a construct of many social circumstances. *There it was*—as if common language itself afforded her mother both manifestations of security in this society, to be at home in it and to be critical of it: "so was liberalism; so was social concern." The integrity of her mother's humane instincts back in the 1920s and after, though of limited effect, might be appreciated more fully by the reader outside of South Africa from a news account such as the following, from many years later, in which we hear a different voice from Gordimer's hometown: On September 14, 1977, at the ruling National party's Transvaal Congress, one day after the black consciousness movement leader Steve Biko died in police custody, allegedly of starvation on a hunger strike (but actually of a beating by the police), a delegate from Springs "drew roars of laughter when he praised the Minister [of Justice] for granting Biko 'his democratic right to starve himself to death.'"[49] How fitting it is that the daughter, living more fully in the English language that was her mother's tongue, has found her own place in the culture, her own critical stance within and against it, as a woman writing in South Africa.

The experiences of her upbringing may have shaped Gordimer's perceptions of gender relations as well, if only by breaking apart the easy dichotomies. In the modest privileges of her background, Nan Myers Gordimer was oddly paired with her husband. While the author identifies her mother as the one sensitive to racial issues, she also recognizes her father's lower social position, his undeveloped and passive personality, and his wife's suppression of his religious practice. We can say, therefore, that despite prospering under an exploitive system to which he acceded, Isidore Gordimer was as unlikely a representative of patriarchal authority as his wife was of patriarchal victimization. He had grown up in an Eastern European village, one of twelve children raised by an elderly relative because his mother and father worked as a dressmaker and a shipping clerk respectively in Riga. With secondary schooling closed to Jews, Isidore was sent alone by boat at the age of thirteen to an uncle who was trying to make his way in South Africa.

Isidore started out as an itinerant watchmaker, repairing the timepieces of miners. By the time his daughters were born, he would be most conveniently described as a jeweler; that term may suggest an image rather grander than the reality in a town like Springs, although he seems to have fared well financially and socially. He gradually became prosperous enough to open a small shop and to pay for nine sisters to immigrate, one by one. His younger daughter, Nadine, revealed, "I found out later that he hated them all—we didn't ever have family gatherings. I don't know why he hated them so much." Like Isidore's place of origin, this aspect of his history was closed off. Even the shtetl's location itself remains somewhat uncertain, beyond what one might expect given the vicissitudes of Baltic boundaries; the rapid loss of contact with origins is exposed in Nadine Gordimer's own confusion; although she had always referred to her father as Lithuanian, in recent years she has noted that his parents actually lived and worked in Riga, and now she identifies him as Latvian.[50] Her own view of her father is of a "timid," "arrested man," without "much of a personality," someone whose character is "still a mystery to me."[51] He seems at any rate to have been someone marked out for endurance, for survival through adaptation. His interrupted adolescence is surely partly accountable for this, but so must be the circumstances in which he found himself in his new country.

Nan Myers Gordimer, though Jewish, came from an assimilated family. Her wedding in Johannesburg's Great Synagogue was also the last service she attended there. In Springs she socialized with Protestant women; both her daughters were sent to a Catholic convent school as day students, although they were excused from religious instruction and worship. Perhaps Mrs. Gordimer's hostility to religion in general was as much a factor in those adjustments as was a desire to shield them from conversionary activity, for Nadine said of her mother that, "if not really an atheist, she certainly was an agnostic, scornful about all organized religions."[52] Because of their mother's outlook, neither Nadine nor her older sister received any Jewish education inside or outside the home, although her adolescent reading afforded her some notion of Jewish experience. The mother's antireligious attitude also affected her husband's life. Isidore, who had received a traditional Jewish upbringing in Eastern Europe, did not continue to practice religion as a married man; his younger child perceived that "my mother more or less forced him to abandon all that." The author remembered, "We kept only the Day of Atonement," and her recollection shows how minimal the "keeping" must have been: "Off he would go to fast— and my sister and I would be sitting in our shorts in the car, waiting for him, looking at these people coming out of the synagogue!"[53] Years later, in a short story called "My Father Leaves Home," the writer constructed a familiar-sounding pattern of religious nonobservances and observances: "If the phylacteries and skullcap were kept somewhere the children never saw them. He went fasting to the synagogue on the Day of Atonement and each year, on the anniversaries of the deaths of the old people in that village whom the wife and children had never seen, went again to light a candle. Feeble flame; who were they? In the quarrels between husband and wife, she saw them as ignorant and dirty" (J, 64).

Nadine Gordimer and her older sister grew up without any religious training in a household devoid of religious observance. Occasional visits to relatives offered contact with what might be called Jewish ethnicity, strange and exotic reminders of Eastern European ways of life. Not only did she have little apparent acquaintance with what "being Jewish" might mean (other than by fundamental differentiation from one's practicing Christian neighbors and classmates), she also missed having imbued the traditional cultural associations, at once potentially enriching and constraining, of being a "Jewish woman," or a "Jewish mother." Her mother was a woman who happened to be Jewish. Also missing from Springs's commercially oriented Jewish environment was Jewish learning. The author would recall later that while exploring the works of Isaac Bashevis Singer in her thirties she was surprised to discover a vibrant Jewish artistic, scholarly, and intellectual culture she had not encountered as she grew up.[54]

We can better grasp from this context why Gordimer's connection with her Jewish family roots does not bear very rich literary fruit. Jewish-oriented material rarely occurs in her writings. She has occasionally drawn upon but not focused on the social world of the South African Jewish community. Only in her first and most strongly autobiographical novel, The Lying Days, do we find a clearly articulated Jewish family environment and someone deeply involved with a Jewish context; revealingly, it is not religion but Zionism that becomes the focus of Jewish identification there. As a national and religious movement concerned with liberation and self-rule for oppressed people, focusing on a certain territory, on a homeland, and on a people's historical ties to that territory, Zionism raises complex issues about ethnic and national identity and, of course, also about roots in the land, subjects relevant to the author herself and to the South African situation in general. Perhaps because the analogies appear so strong yet the equations and lessons so unclear, Gordimer and her characters seem not to have commented specifically on Zionism since *The Lying Days*. In *A Sport of Nature*, however, Hillela (Jewish in origin but married to an African head of state) is photographed with the perennially smiling Yassir Arafat, as the author briefly registers modern African politics responding to the conflict between Palestinians and Israel.

Still, one can speculate that being sensitive to the status of Jews in her country has possibly helped her comprehend those who feel excluded or who cannot participate in the collective beliefs or pieties expressed around them; it has also perhaps raised her awareness of arbitrary injustice in the treatment of other people. A suggestive passage in *Occasion for Loving* links Jewish consciousness with the outsider's consciousness. Jessie, the protagonist, takes her children to a Christmas-morning service at a black township Anglican church. They are accompanied by Boaz, a family friend who is Jewish but wants to hear the choir.

> He did not kneel when the rest of them did, but all the time sat with repose, listening to the flock of voices that rose steeply around him, or the low sound of prayer. All through the ritual of Christmas, the curious swarming of the human spirit, some of it meaningless, some meaningful, he had given and partaken with zest and a pleasure in participation. Yet from time to time, as now, although she was kneeling and he was a respectful onlooker, she was aware of something that set them apart together. She, a Christian, assumed with her husband and others a common experience of the Christmas ritual, along with other common experiences. But the truth was that for her the common experience was not there. . . . Behind the kissing and the laughter and the exchange of presents, there was his Jewishness (*OL*, 45–46).

Christmas is an appropriate focal point for such consciousness of one's relationship to an experience that is not merely religious but more broadly cultural. To Boaz, the event is "sound" that occurs around him. While he joins in the merriment with good will, he cannot participate in the full experience. His detachment derives from his being Jewish, yet the experience of alienation is not uniquely Jewish, as we understand from Jessie's thought that she and he are "apart together." For other reasons she too feels estranged, behind the "assumed . . . common experience." Boaz's presence as someone who is and is not a part of this scene allows her to recognize that in herself. Perhaps in the dyadic alienation embodied in these two characters we can recognize the poles of the author's upbringing, as someone raised in Christian social settings and educated in a parochial school, yet knowing that she was Jewish and consequently detached from the "common experience."

The same book suggests one of the levels of connection between Jews and other oppressed people. When Gideon, the black African lover of Boaz's wife, is with Ann, he "forgot he was an African, burdened, like a Jew, with his category of the chosen" (OL, 141). It is significantly perceptive that the author comprehends the Jew's "chosenness" as a burden rather than a privilege or source of pride. Indeed, this may be the most tellingly Jewish insight in her fiction. Later in the novel, when Jessie describes Boaz's personality as "perhaps a bit of the natural victim's," it is hard to say whether "natural" refers to him as an individual or as a Jew (OL, 266). The Lying Days attests that in the social structure of a 1940s South African mining town, the Jews were the lowest category of whites because they were the merchants who dealt regularly with blacks in some capacity other than authoritarian; to their white compatriots, exogenous marriage with a Jew would be an act of rashness worthy of sympathy. As the Jewish ANC leader Joe Slovo (himself an immigrant from Lithuania) has remarked, "I think the Jewish population had a great sense of insecurity because they were a minority in the white population (now some 110,000 out of 5 million), faced with a regime with anti-Semitic tendencies. . . . The people who normally join a liberation movement must have been influenced in some cases . . . against the background of the treatment of Jews generally, racism against Jews." [55]

In her fiction, Gordimer has certainly acknowledged Jews' almost stereotypical participation in liberal causes, in the liberation movement, in cultural activities, and in the professions. Although it would be wrong to overstate that involvement in Gordimer's fiction or in South African life as a whole, one certainly cannot ignore the prominence among antiapartheid activists of people like the author herself, the stalwart liberal parliamentarian Helen Suzman, Slovo and his late wife, Ruth First (killed by a mail bomb in 1983 while in exile), or the ANC activists who fell victim to the same roundup at Livonia that resulted in Nelson Mandela's and Walter Sisulu's arrests, including Lionel Bernstein, Dennis Goldberg, Arthur Goldreich and Harold Wolpe. In My Son's Story the cultural contributions of German Jews to life in a small mining town are noted (on page sixteen) through narrative asides that may seem rather gratuitous, except that they appropriately expand the reader's recognition of South Africa's multicultural heritage. More strikingly, in the same novel the protagonist's lawyer seems to embody all the favorable stereotypically Jewish characteristics in one individual: "Metkin looked like a rabbi and listened as his client thought a psychiatrist would listen," combining "contemporary and ancient wisdom, divination" (*MSS*, 158).

Jewish identification can be distinguished from Jewish identity. Growing up estranged from Jewish life and practice, taught nothing of Jewish history, Gordimer has not had this culture as part of her life. Though she was in her early twenties when World War II ended and the concentration camp newsreels appeared (with such an impact on the Jewish identification of so many otherwise-assimilated Jews, for example, the American poet Adrienne Rich, six years younger and part Jewish), Gordimer seems scarcely to have alluded to the Holocaust in her fiction or essays, notwithstanding the European background of her father and many of her characters. Indeed, the one story specifically about refugees from Hitler's Germany ("Face from Atlantis," published in the early 1950s) is devoted to non-Jewish emigrees, whose optimism and nostalgia are surely validated precisely because they and their families did not have to deal with the realities of the death camps. In a work from the 1991 collection, a white political fugitive who has written a phone number on his wrist thinks later (with no particular ethnic focus) that it "was a frivolous travesty of the brand concentration-camp survivors keep of their persecution" ("Safe Houses," *J*, 194). One of the ironies of Gordimer's career—and at the same time a fact that should caution against pat assumptions about modern Jewish experience and the mental worlds of writers—is that when she became the first woman in twenty-five years to win the Nobel Prize for Literature, her most immediate predecessor was another Jew, the poet Nelly Sachs, whose best-known works are intense elegies on the Holocaust, which she narrowly escaped, and religious poetry suffused with her knowledge of Jewish mystical and spiritual writings. Another irony is that among Gordimer's numerous other literary honors was the German prize (awarded in 1986) named for Sachs, a writer with whom Gordimer seems to have so little in common artistically except for her Jewish origins and, perhaps most importantly and appropriately, serious ethical commitments.

Still, not only is Gordimer's distance from Jewish culture and religion understandable given her background, the void of Jewish identity is especially understandable given her attempt to make an African consciousness for herself. Since the right-wing opposition to majority rule always derides "tribalism" among black Africans and cites it as a destabilizing factor should black people receive full political rights and economic justice, critics like Gordimer have insisted on pointing out tribalism among the Afrikaners and English. In this context, Jewish ethnicity could be resisted as simply another tribal manifestation, imposed from the outside and obscuring the indigenous cultures whose tribal integrity and value have not been respected. The main character in *A Sport of Nature*, Hillela (whose name must evoke, among other associations, the great rabbi Hillel) does come from a nominally Jewish family, but family connections and the received traditions of the past are included among the identities from which she liberates herself.

More broadly, we might notice that despite the importance of some religious leaders in the liberation struggle (Desmond Tutu, Alan Boesak, and Beyers Naudé being merely the most widely known), Gordimer rarely depicts a scene in which a representative of an organized church plays a significant role. (There are, to be sure, exceptions, but they are revealing: for example, Father Mayekiso, who delivers prayers at a graveside demonstration in *My Son's Story*, is a noble presence, but in a walk-on role.) The most notable moments of religious or spiritual observance are ones like the ending of *The Conservationist*, where the African farm workers gather to rebury a slain African in a traditional Zulu rite that both returns him to African soil and claims that land for him as an African. Though at least one reader has tried to apply familiar Christian symbolism to the resurrection motif in this book, that seems distortive, even though Gordimer's range of reading and her early education at the convent school of Our Lady of Mercy certainly would have exposed her to the main elements of Christian symbolism.[56] It would be a mistake to overlook the element of spirituality in Gordimer's work, but her spiritual inspirations do not assume Christian forms. If they take specific shape, the shapes of African traditions seem to her at least as good as any because of the bond with the land.

Gordimer has explained that, while neither adhering to any particular body of belief nor evoking artistically familiar Christian symbology, "I have a basically religious temperament, perhaps even a profoundly religious one." That is said notwithstanding her description of herself as an atheist. Gordimer's spirituality seems founded on a conviction that beneath the particular cultural manifestations of our languages, traditions, and ethnicities, we share a oneness of essential humanity. Too often we are blocked from perceiving and acting on this by the political and economic interests that manipulate us; consequently, our separateness aids our exploitation. Thus, the religious temperament manifests itself in her work through characters who feel that underlying union, committing themselves to it as their faith.

We may find, consequently, a tension in Gordimer's self-identification between the universalism implied by her spiritual, socialist political outlook on the one hand and the particularism of her African self-identification on the other. Yet, to say this is only to admit in her work and thought the double awareness to which every construct of faith and belief leads us. By tracing how Gordimer's sense of herself as an African developed, we can appreciate more fully how that led her beyond the personal or private to a broader identification with humankind.

CHAPTER TWO

OUT OF SPRINGS

We pause at this image, taken by Gordimer's collaborator, the photographer David Goldblatt: Straight legs trimly tapering en pointe, an unnamed young white girl (let us guess just into her teens), exultant before her audience, strikes a classic pose with her slender long arms arching upward in fifth position, "on the stoep of her parents' house, Boksburg, 1980." The ample marbled terrazzo tiles make up her stage floor; her backdrop is the neat subtropical geometry of white walls, lace-curtained windows, and porch shadows. The white iron chairs just visible at stage left stand in for courtiers or the set designer's balustrade. The ballerina from a Petipa "white" ballet has pirouetted here, out of context, but graciously happy to perform.

She is displaying her new tutu; her hair, pulled straight back, lies slick in performance-ready tightness, while a floral bow visible at the back of her head secures what might be a French braid. Her toothy smile reveals a missing molar. Behind those closed eyes—lids shut perhaps against the sun, though one imagines her teacher saying, "No, dear, just modestly lowered," and wishing the elbows weren't quite so sharp—her parents and this stranger behind the camera are not her only audience, wherever it is that she sees herself, and how. Somewhere beyond here, she moves in the dynamic energy of what she takes to be her own freedom.[1]

"I wanted to be a dancer," Nadine Gordimer once told an interviewer; "This was my passion, from the age of about four to ten. I absolutely adored dancing. . . . There was no question but that I was to be a dancer, and I suppose maybe I would have been."[2] What put an end to that exuberant movement and feeling of personal power were an enlarged thyroid that caused a rapid heartbeat and her mother's decision when the condition was discovered to keep her daughter from all physical activity and eventually to take her out of school, effectively separating the lively girl from contact with other children. A few years later, at twenty, Gordimer knew that this allegedly debilitating abnormality was minor, insignificant. Another ten years later, she had a deeper comprehension of the motives, which she would probe publicly only after her mother's 1976 death. Gordimer acknowledged that the reason for this extraordinary, callous decision was that by keeping her younger daughter at home, Nan Gordimer obtained a companion for herself in an unhappy marriage and sustained a close social relationship (Gordimer convincingly interprets it as an unconscious attraction) with the family doctor, who became a frequent visitor. For a year the child was at home, and then, until she was about fifteen (the exact age varies in interviews) she was sent to a tutor for three hours a day, time principally spent doing assignments by herself. "So the dancing stopped like that."[3] Among the other consequences of this adolescence was that when she was ready to study more broadly in her early twenties, without a school diploma she could only take occasional courses as an extramural student, which she did for a year at the University of Witwatersrand, one of the most politically liberal universities in the country.

The unintentionally cruel, selfishly motivated isolation imposed by her mother may have helped Gordimer become a writer.[4] Implying the connection herself, she has recently remarked, "But [my mother] did this, so that meant I was home a great deal; and I think it was then that I began to write."[5] Apparently earlier, though, captivated by Evelyn Waugh's *Scoop*, the dance-smitten girl had thought that she "also" wanted to be a journalist and so had already been interested in writing. Given this predeliction, having the time and the need to express energy, imagination, and freedom may well lead to a more earnest involvement with writing or at least scribbling. Still, it is irresistible to contrast her remark with the more confident (and resentful) assertion by the narrator, Will, in *My Son's Story* (a book published two years after this statement), who claims about another sort of parental treachery, "What he did—my father—made me a writer" (*MSS*, 277). Will's allegation does seem too simple on the face of it. Yet in the distance between these two formulations we register the difference between having the opportunity and desire "to write" and becoming "a writer."

To hear the rhythms of sentences, to get the shape and heft of words, even to know what and who are worth telling about are not the by-products of parental subterfuges and insufficiently hidden secrets or hypocrisies. Yet it is true that perceiving such deceptions can lead one to probe the nature of the gaps separating self from other, the public appearance from the private reality, the inner experience of living among others while knowing that one is at odds with what must be shown them. Such knowledge can also increase one's interest in how one constructs appearances and evades admissions, that is, how rhetorical and narrative strategies function to constitute our images of what we are and what we believe in.

The storytelling began early for Gordimer, who was first published in the children's supplement of a Johannesburg newspaper when she was thirteen years old; her first story about adults appeared at fifteen. Could anything so consuming have ever been thought of as a pastime? How else did she spend her time in those lonely years without the companionship of other children? Her sister, four years older, was already away at the university.

She certainly read enthusiastically, relying especially on the public library. (Later, as a public figure addressing the future of South Africa, Gordimer would write passionately, as we have noted, on the need for libraries and bookstores, as well as better schools, in black communities, stressing the essential role of the free public library, which had been closed to blacks, in her own education.) Reading meant feeding not only on prose but also on ideas. For although much of her time was spent in the company of adults, going to tea parties with her mother and to dinner engagements with both parents, the conversations in such circumstances were trivial; they are likely to be so under most circumstances, but this is particularly the case in a community such as the one in which she was born (on November 20, 1923) and raised. In Springs, a Transvaal gold-mining town about forty miles east of Johannesburg, many of the other people of the Gordimers' social class were merchants from the same background as her father, poorly educated Jewish immigrants from the shtetls of Latvia and Lithuania making a decent but modest living.

The future author also developed a talent for mimicry, no doubt the product of those hours spent listening to the grown-ups and watching them, herself apparently (for it is always only apparently) unseen.[6] As an adult she judged that such liberty makes a child "a kind of jester, an entertainer for grownups," but one could also say that in compensation it grants the artist-in-training (for so a jester can be) permission to expose the manners and mannerisms of others with impunity and be rewarded for it, if only with praise. She recalled, "I . . . contented myself with mimicking, for the entertainment of one group of my parents' friends, other friends who were not present. It did not seem to strike those who were that, in their absence, they would change places with the people they were laughing at; or perhaps it did, I do them an injustice, and they didn't mind."[7] But there was more than praise; there was license (which, as Milton pointed out, is not exactly the same as liberty). "Adults find you charming. You flirt with other people's husbands instead of with boys your own age. It's a very corrupting thing." Those are judgments that would come later, along with the rigor of moral perception, whose origin cannot be neatly found. It is that rigor we discern as Gordimer appraises the effect on her own adolescent character ("A child like that becomes very corrupt"), or even more pointedly when she first derides her audience (whom "it did not seem to strike") for their impercipience then tentatively vindicates their generosity while criticizing her own previous condescension toward them. As precise as Gordimer can be in seeming to delineate "this is what it was like," the descriptive and evocative passages about the past are not left to themselves. They will be held to account, even the unexamined life the writer once lived. One may suspect that such exacting measure of behavior arises from grasping early the damage that can be done when people are dishonest to themselves and others.

Gordimer was born in South Africa, but although the child of Jewish immigrants, she made herself an African. Her maternal grandparents had come from England. Her grandfather, a hard-living trader, remained in South Africa, but her grandmother returned to England shortly before her daughter Nan was born, not returning to South Africa until the child was six.[8] The family found in South Africa some measure of the prosperity they had sought in making that voyage during the boom years of the 1890s, the father succeeding as a small trader on the stock exchange. Receiving what the writer described as a "good education in Johannesburg," Gordimer's mother had, as we have seen, the social advantages of acculturation as well as middle-class status; furthermore, English was her native tongue.[9] Indeed, Nan Gordimer and those among whom she made her social circle (often Scots Presbyterians) continued to speak of England as "home."[10] Yet that home was a place to which they did not go. Life in Africa could be made to resemble that of an English town, but it still entailed the colonial experience of living amid and "above" the indigenous peoples.

However such feelings were inculcated, Nan Gordimer possessed the decency and awareness divinely commanded to the religious tradition that she stifled in her husband and omitted from her daughters' education: to "know the heart of the stranger, for you were strangers in the land of Egypt." Nadine Gordimer has come to reject the political worth of humanistic individualism—her mother's belief that one has made a sufficient political benefaction simply by personally treating other people civilly and performing good works for them. Still, that maternal example of regarding even the generally despised African blacks as simply other human beings toward whom one had the moral obligations of common decency as well as some practical responsibilities of charity was undoubtedly significant in affording Nadine a place from which to begin developing a more sophisticated social and political consciousness.

For the young Gordimer, that expanded commitment became possible after she started moving in Johannesburg's literary, musical, and artistic circles in 1949. Her previous contact with blacks was confined to servants and mineworkers, whose situation could arouse in her pity, compassion, and awareness of injustice but perhaps little more. In Springs, "the mineworkers themselves, not knowing the language, feeling rather timid, felt a lack of proper understanding even of the simple purchase of something." [11] As appropriate and important as the feelings of pity, compassion, and justice might be in allowing her to go beyond the sequestrations of emotions and identity instilled by her local environment while growing up, they could not allow her to comprehend what full equality could mean. At exuberant parties and public gatherings in Johannesburg, she interacted intellectually and socially with black people who, though still oppressed by the laws and customs of the country, knew the language, were not timid (and in some cases were intimidated by no one), blacks who were the peers of educated whites in knowledge, intelligence, and talents. [12] At that stage Gordimer began to understand herself as more fully an African. It was also in 1949 that she published her first collection of stories, *Face to Face*. It can be said appropriately that her emergence as an artist began around the time of her emergence as a more socially aware person and that since those beginnings these two aspects of her work and life have been joined through their mutual developments.

In virtual counterpoint through a prolific career, Gordimer has alternated volumes of short stories with novels:

1952	*The Soft Voice of the Serpent and Other Stories*
1953	*The Lying Days*
1956	*Six Feet of the Country* (stories)
1958	*A World of Strangers*
1960	*Friday's Footprint and Other Stories*
1963	*Occasion for Loving*
1965	*Not for Publication and Other Stories*
1966	*The Late Bourgeois World*
1970	*A Guest of Honour*
1971	*Livingstone's Companions* (stories)
1973	*The Black Interpreters: Notes on African Writing* and *On the Mines*, an essay for David Goldblatt's photographs
1974	*The Conservationist*
1975	*Selected Stories*
1976	*Some Monday for Sure* (stories)

young man sitting
the lion, fallen
of the phys
have ca
not

Looking at such a list, one can see how full
has been. A story occasionally evokes the i
have led to a novel. Perhaps maintaining clos
has helped keep the novels focused on the vi   ... vi-
gnette or set piece that sharpens our percep   ...acter or theme.
Gordimer's two collaborations with David Goldblatt (1986's *Lifetimes:
Under Apartheid*, with selections from her published fiction accompanying
his photographs, and *On the Mines*) demonstrate how important the
caught moment, exemplified by the visual image, is in her writing. She has
said herself that her narrative ability developed some years into her career,
after she had established a substantial reputation based on other literary
gifts, one of the most prominent being the descriptive.

In her writing, however, *descriptive* in fact rarely means *pictorial*. We
may get to know, through occasional details, something of what a character
looks like or wears, and we will get rather more of the physical makeup of
rooms or natural settings, but the work rarely seems to pause while the
author describes a picture for us. Gordimer knows the difference between
the literary and the pictorial; actually, examining the collaborations with
Goldblatt, we perceive that his photographs and her texts may be thematically connected, but the one does not illustrate or describe the other. Text
and photograph seem more generally complementary in the way that both
media place individuals within succinctly evoked social as well as physical
contexts.

In Gordimer's fiction, description emerges not in set pieces but through
the layering of details built up over the course of the story or novel, emerging out of a sustained awareness of milieu and social conduct and relationship, the eye keen for the telling gesture or physical detail, just as the ear
is alert to the turn of speech. So in a story from the 1952 collection, "The
Train From Rhodesia," a woman's rage over her husband's successful, ag-
gressive bargaining with an African woodcarver leaves the couple silent in
the railway car along with their beautiful forlorn trophy, the three figures
themselves like a sculptural grouping: "Smuts blew in grittily, settled on
her hands. Her back remained at exactly the same angle, turned against the

with his hands drooping between his sprawled legs, and on its side in the corner" (*Sel*, 55). That expressive power ... is what the writer notices, what Goldblatt's photographs ... within personal, South African relationships. Again, he does ... illustrate her work so much as illuminate the precise consciousness of ... place within which her work can be more clearly understood. For those of us among Gordimer's readers who have never seen South Africa ourselves, his pictures (like her writings) do something rather different for us than the travelogue illustrations of Table Bay and bougainvillea in bloom, but they also do something different from the news pictures of rumbling armored Casspirs, of sjamboks and truncheons flailing at dodging figures scrambling in the dust, or the activists' slides setting lush suburban Johannesburg beside the dense squalor of neighboring black townships like Alexandria and the morose huts in a waste and barren Ciskei.

Consider, for instance, another of Goldblatt's pictures.

"Farmer's son with his nursemaid, Marico Bushveld, 1964."[13] That much, only, the caption tells us. The figures are in the foreground, facing us but in semiprofile next to a small tree whose main branches curve upward like fingers balancing an egg. She is seated on a ring of concrete protectively surrounding the tree; he stands just behind her with his hands on her back. They are separated from the field and the softly mounded, tree-covered hill by a line of chicken-wire fencing topped by barbed wire. He looks about six years old, a barefooted, healthy-cheeked, lean white boy in dark shorts, intensely white patterned shirt, and beaked dark cap, head tilted as if against the glare, squinting at the camera with his mouth stretched into what an unwilling child of his age takes as a passable substitute for a smile. She is perhaps in her late teens, a dark African with firm jaw, close-cropped hair, a knit halter top showing in profile the point of a young breast, and print skirt draped midway down her thigh, exposing her strong-looking bare legs and feet. Her face, exactly at the focal center of the photograph, smiles with perfect close-mouthed self-composure across her right shoulder at the viewer, eyes open, candid in their gaze. That face, that look of almost-amused consciousness of the presence out here, would arrest the most casual passerby.

The boy's far hand seems to lie gently on her left shoulder; his right rests with the tips touching her shoulder strap, but a pale fingernail against the dark semicircle indicates how his index finger just finds the skin of her back. It is so unthinkingly domestic, so easily familiar, that touch—absent of anxiety, of tension, of any meaning, yet, deeper than a child's cozy reliance on the one who takes care of him, who cares for him. And perhaps one notices then something odd at his left foot. Looking more *closely, one sees what that is: She has reached back with her hand—her nursemaid's hand—clasping it around the back of his heel, her palm gripping his foot as they pose for their picture. It is a gesture of such exquisite, tender intimacy that one's breath catches.*

Like such pictures, Gordimer's stories and novels call to our eye and ear the precise ways in which we touch one another and frame our comprehension of those ways within an interpretive context of race, class, and gender. When the author claims in her essays that apartheid (among its other offenses) denies the truth that black and white South Africans have grown up alongside one another, not actually separate but in conditions of physical and even emotional proximity that are indeed unequal but intimate nonetheless, doubtless she draws on moments of familiarity such as this one that Goldblatt has caught.[14]

To say that it is on this level of understanding that Gordimer's writing expresses the political is not to deny the power of ethical conviction and political comprehension that she brings to public issues. Nor need one ignore the fact that in her novels characters do engage in overt discussion of social and political theories, as well as realities. The approach of most of her novels could be described by words used with regard to *A Guest of Honour:* "I tried to write a political novel treating the political theme as personally as a love story."[15] It is worth stressing that she has not merely spoken of treating the political as a love story, but something literarily more acute, as *personally* as a love story. In brief, although characters live within and speak from a particular biographical context that allows them to articulate a specific way of thinking about social and political issues, we do not experience them as simply allegorical figures or mouthpieces. Even when we may feel that a particular character is being set up for exposure or criticism, we are compelled to comprehend the person along with the condemnation.

Perhaps one reason why this is so is that Gordimer remembers her own past, her own history, and forces herself to acknowledge, to attest that she herself has been silent about injustices, at times unaware, at other times aware but unconscious of the meaning, at still other times aware and conscious but lacking the means to interpret the act. Stephen Clingman noted that in *The Lying Days,* which is set in South Africa during the late 1940s, the protagonist thinks with romantic admiration of the 1922 strike by white miners, but the book does not mention the brutally suppressed 1946 strike by 60,000 members of the black African Mineworkers Union, which resulted in the deaths of a dozen miners. Of this event, Gordimer told Clingman, she would hardly have been aware.[16] Not for much longer would she be capable of such obliviousness to contemporary politics in South Africa, but she recalls that at that time she was, and she knows that the trajectory of her awareness has not been followed by most other South African whites.

The changing awareness has been effected in two ways. One, as indicated above, was through the acquisition of wider experience, especially about race, than Springs had permitted her. The other was through the acquisition of understanding. With the ambitious eclecticism of the self-educated, she has read not only world literature but also works in the social sciences, in politics and economics, and in psychology and sociology; in so doing she has developed a significant grasp of the theoretical and practical issues of power. What is rare is that these take on "a local habitation and a name" in her prose without substituting for the art. Her characters sometimes argue about doctrinal issues and fall out with one another over tactics and strategies, but we are always returned to how those disagreements, reassessments, and changes in hierarchy express themselves in the timing of a gesture, the phrasing of a remark, the qualities of sexual contact. We can see all of these in the following passages from *My Son's Story* as characters respond to a protagonist's political fall.

> That's how it goes, Sonny, a damned shame. . . . Some people (a shake of the head), *aie!* you can't trust them, they're too ambitious and you're too straight. . . . You know what I mean? When he confronted Hannah, together with whom, since the first discovery of this possibility between them, every political question had been analysed, she wasn't able to employ the faculty—not this time, not for this. All she could do was comfort him, touch him and enfold him, her soft thighs clamped heavily over his body, her arms tight around his neck, hands thrust into his hair, as if she were gathering him up and putting him together again. (*MSS*, 200)

Gordimer shows us how much such details express in any interaction between people. In particular between races in her country, these details are part of a multilevel communication in which the unsaid or undone cannot be overlooked. There is always a subtext.

An episode from *A World of Strangers* can illustrate this. The narrator, Toby, is a young Englishman from a leftist literary family working in his family's business in South Africa. Less absorbed with activism than his family and less doctrinaire in his social activity, he still pursues friendships with blacks and chafes against South African racism. Toby's liberalism, which is not radicalism, is reflected not only in his choice of friends (a matter of personal affinity) but also in his casual dealings with other black people, especially servants. On a hunting trip, while cut off from the others, he happens upon one of the African doghandlers who has also gotten separated. Toby's "I'm lost too" casually puts them on the same footing, while his subsequent "I don't think we should just keep on walking, do you?" is a tiny model of political interaction, as if this were a consultation under some scheme for racially cooperative development; the white man states a clearly directive opinion, apparently inviting his black partner's viewpoint though actually soliciting concurrence, which comes passively: "He stood there with the dog and said nothing (WS, 244). Mentally oriented by his background toward seeing experience in political terms but personally resistant of political activism (which he, as an outsider here, does have the luxury of eschewing, notwithstanding his and his family's economic involvement with the country), Toby attempts to relate to the African as if they were equal individuals.

That they are not equals becomes manifest through the marginal interaction between them. Not responding to the white man's speech unless it is a direct question, not looking "at me or at anything" (WS 245), declining to remove a proferred cigarette from the white man's pack, the African seems to exist someplace different from his white temporary companion. Were the two men of the same race and social equals in the way that Toby would have it, such behavior might simply mark a taciturn nature; "his isolation . . . must have existed all the time." Toby's observation that "he and I were in hand's reach of each other, like people standing close, and unaware of it, in a fog" suggests private noncommunication, the Forsterian failure to "connect" on the personal level as individuals. They are disconnected, however, by social conditions, as we are reminded when, later that night, the men entertain themselves around two different campfires, singing or joking in their own ways in their own languages, the whites with their red wine, the blacks with their ration of brandy ("Kaffirs don't really like wine," [WS, 239]) provided by their white bosses.

The choice of narrator for this work indicates one of the principal methods by which Gordimer has both freed herself from her own socialized contextualization and expressed a methodology of growth leading to commitment and liberation. The need to gain understanding by looking at experience through someone's else's eyes is almost axiomatic. Gordimer's use of narrative strategies throughout her works is expressive of that. Even though he forms a romance with a white South African woman and a couple of strong friendships with black African men, Toby seems to be visiting "a world of strangers," not really living with them. (That they are also strangers from one another is a fact we will consider later in this chapter.) While this book is about how South Africa may look from the outsider's vantage point, it is also a book about the impossibility of an outsider truly being inside that country. Paradoxically, then, the book marks its author's national self-consciousness (one cannot call it nationalism) even as it attests (through the other implicit meaning in Toby's status) to Gordimer's conscious estrangement from it.

Writing the book through the eyes and voice of a man from England is not the most daring feat of her narrative ventriloquism. Probably even more striking is Mehring's narration in *The Conservationist*, for he is a crass, selfish, sexually predatory, arrogant, and powerful businessman playing out a romantic infatuation with his newly purchased Transvaal farmland. By forcing us, as Gordimer must have forced herself, to listen to such a man, to comprehend how he imagines people and places, what he notices and overlooks, how he judges and evaluates, the author compels us to cross the boundary of judgment whose borders we, no less than anyone else, are likely to accept as safely inviolable. Mehring's analytic shrewdness of appraisal and suspicion exempts himself only, until the end. As the author moves in and out of Mehring's consciousness, his narrative point of view generally predominates; his arrogant ego dissects and mocks the motives and honesty of everyone. He sees through them all, usually with a contemptuous assessment, occasionally with a grudging approval intermingling with calculation, an attitude reflecting his critical distance from whomever he *observes* even while seeming to interact with them. Mehring's exploring of what this land might mean to him and our developing consciousness of the psychosexual urges that connect him with it lead to some of the most lyrical, expressly descriptive, time-stopping passages in all of Gordimer's work. These are not narrated by Mehring but rather seem to come from a consciousness more subtle, more authorial than his and yet directed by what has caught his attention. So our vision extends beyond Mehring. Still, granted we may not like him more, we will feel much deeper understanding of him, even compassion for him. Without becoming an apologist for him, by truly exposing him through (among other ways) his own words and actions even as she makes him comprehensible, the author has led us to "connect" with him, breaking those barriers of feeling, understanding, and identification that are the essential mental and emotional structures created by apartheid.

Although experimentation with multiple narrators and floating or indefinite narrative perspectives are certainly facets of modern fiction in general and contemporary fiction in particular (elements that take the author outside the traditional borders of purely "realistic" fiction), as these comments suggest, it would be wrong to interpret Gordimer's increasing use of these techniques from *The Conservationist* onward as a purely literary strategy. Fully understanding the epistemological implications, she shows multiple meanings as events are seen or narrated from different viewpoints, articulated in different voices. That does not mean that ethical judgment yields to the apparently implied subjectivity of all experience, however.

Those multiple perspectives deny the "privilege" of the individual vantage point, the liberal humanistic confidence in the subjective rightness or validity of the single consciousness. When those different voices speak out of significantly differing experiential contexts, we learn instead that to understand actions we must understand how they are understood by and affect others. Moral accountability is suggested, therefore, by the forced consciousness of the other. Being denied even the self-protective comfort of a stable narrative angle of vision, we are made open to new understanding, re-vision. Comprehending the story may mean knowing what it is like from different viewpoints, by a sort of democratization of the narration, a literary analogue of political change.

The story "What Were You Dreaming?" (in *Jump*), for example, begins with a first-person interior monologue and indirect dialogue narrated by a "Cape Coloured" hitchhiker. After he is picked up by two white people and falls asleep in the back seat of their car, this narrative viewpoint gives way to a third-person narrator who conveys the thoughts and conversation of the whites, an earnest visiting Englishman and an older, knowledgeable South African woman who has been showing the tourist her country with some annoyance at how little he knew before and how slowly he is grasping what he sees and hears. By beginning with the hitchhiker's keen analytic perspective on them and his careful gauging of who they are and what he can say to them, the author compels us to hear their conversation in his context. Even more significantly, he has acquired a presence for us independent of their judgments and analysis of him. He is not simply an object to be talked about, dozing in the back seat, and when they leave him—"anywhere," he insists, because the buses don't run on Sundays—we admit the truth of the woman's sense that she is the one "accountable" but without disregarding the Englishman's polite and well-intentioned miscomprehension of ordinary life here or our own sense that we have had a glimpse into something sullied, sullying.

Narrative strategy acquires more than usual significance when our awareness is heightened of who is seeing, telling, and being heard, a fact not confined to one country or to the particular issue of race relations. In much the same way, one senses how the meaning of language usage is highly determined by cultural factors. We become specially attuned to recognizing not only who is telling the story but also in what language and at what linguistic level. To begin with, the language one speaks and the accent in which one speaks it have special complexities in South Africa because of the differing histories, alliances, hostilities, and ethnic outlooks of the multitude of linguistically distinct peoples comprising the country (Xhosa, Zulu, Afrikaans, Venda, Sotho, and English, for a sampling), complicated by immigrations, migrations, minglings, and intermarriages. As we have noted earlier in regard to Gordimer's own family, the language difference has a way of underscoring other differences. What occurred in the family also took place regularly in the interactions between the Springs shopkeepers and the miners:

> I would walk up past these stores, and I would see the storekeepers coming out, themselves rather bewildered, immigrants who knew the language slightly, or who'd learnt it imperfectly, both English and Afrikaans, and who felt alien. Then their customers were, again, people who had come to a country they didn't know . . . a very different part of Africa, usually, from the part they came from. Now these two people, the storekeeper and his customer, understood each other very badly . . . the mineworkers themselves, not knowing the language. . . . So the relationships tended to be rough, people shouting at each other.[17]

The linguistic relationship, in other words, replicated the political: The storekeepers, themselves at the bottom of the white social hierarchy, would "regard [the miners] as absolute savages."

The native's ear becomes finely tuned to speech nuances, not necessarily even for subtleties of connotation but for the cruder necessities of denotation. In "What Were You Dreaming," though the English visitor wants to converse with the hitchhikers he imprudently insists on picking up, they do not understand his British accent, answer him with "a deaf man's guess at what's called for," and "embarrass him" by calling him *baas* and *master*, as they have learned to do. He, on the other hand, hasn't realized that this passenger is not black until his companion asks him the question verifying he has failed another test, "From the way he speaks English—couldn't you hear he's not like the Africans you've talked to?" (J 218).

In addition to the large distinctions carried by language or accent, subtleties of terminology (what identifiable group is marginalized and denigrated by being called a tribe, for instance) indicate not simply what something is but also where the speaker's place is. Given a government that, without a trace of irony, can title a law expanding the system of identification papers required of black inhabitants as the "Abolition of Passes and Coordination of Documents Act" or that can name a police agency the "Bureau of State Security" and thereby give it the acronym BOSS, how could a writer avoid focusing attention on the politics of terminology?

So, for example, when Mehring in *The Conservationist* hears his son refer to Namibia (rather than South-West Africa), he asks, "Why do you call it 'Namibia'?" and understands that he is making a fine distinction through his own phrasing. Mehring thinks that with his leftist ex-lover, he might have raised the conceptually argumentative question, "Why call it 'Namibia'?" meaning, why accept that politically conceived term rather than any of the other words that might more accurately name what the place is like, who lives there, or where it is? The seemingly small difference of wording in the question he has asked his son really means, why do *you* take on the cause of territorial independence by preferring that name (*CN*, 132)? Consciousness about language, that is to say, carries with it consciousness about the differences between the verbal or intellectual constructs of a world and the real lived experience. Here, too, Gordimer has dramatized the essential dialogue between lived and perceived reality.

It is by participating in that dialogue that one comes to know oneself. The course of Gordimer's novels can be seen as traversing the lives of characters dealing with selfhood, the identification of who they are as individuals and as members of society within the particular contexts of their historical and social situations. This is not an essentialist view of "the human condition" or "the nature of man." Rather, it sees that what we are cannot be separated from what we say and do in the conditions with which we are living or against which we are living. Four centuries ago Sir Philip Sidney articulated the notion that "poetry" (by which he meant imaginative literature or "art") combines the best aspects of philosophy and history and is therefore superior to both: It remedies philosophy's defect of abstractness by embodying ideas in situations and history's defect of particularity by showing the meaning of those situations. Again, a photograph by David Goldblatt affords a pictorial analogue to Gordimer's balance of philosophy and history, of conceptual grasp and specificity of incident.

The composition has almost the static formality of a Renaissance engraving, a study in perspective and balance. Two male figures, the left one taller and more massive, face one another in the foreground, channeling our gaze into the central section of the photograph. Distant, in the middle at the vanishing point, a tiny figure stands isolated; much nearer, and positioned closer to the smaller figure, another man poses in contrapposto, *facing toward us. The simple setting, a sparse expanse of plowed earth, with a low hill ridge running across the background, offers no distractions from the human scene.*

The larger man is white, casually dressed but wearing a sport coat. The coat stretches against the solid pack of his middle-aged body, top button pulling and sleeves x-creased as if rumpled through long days behind steering wheels. His close-sheared hair completes the squared look of his head; the little ear, almost lobeless and set far back across the broad expanse of cheek, seems to be an afterthought. His mouth is open in speech, the corners tucked tightly.

The black man looking at the other man's face (though with body slightly angled toward the camera) wears a cap resembling a seventeenth-century helmet, its sloping brim inscribing a gentle S between its own coal-black shadow and a perfectly flat and toneless sky. He smiles broadly as he looks up to the taller white man. Shoulders set back, the black man seems to be leaning slightly away, toward the near right. Between them, the fourth figure is another black man in farm-laborer's clothes, his shoes and lower pants legs caked in mud, pausing with the white cylinder of a cigarette dangling from the corner of his mouth, cap beak pulled over his forehead, eyes down. Too far back to be included in what is being said, he is like a corresponding image for the person on this side of the picture, the one taking or looking at it; the figure in the center is a silent witness.

The event, if we may call it that, is taking place between those two, the bulky solid-shouldered white man, barely contained by his coat, talking out of a taut and unsmiling mouth, and the behatted black man in his sweater and workpants, leaning away as he looks up smiling, smiling to the white man's face. It is a double portrait: "Farmer, Johannes van der Linde, with his head labourer, Ou Sam, near Bloemfontein, 1965."[18]

For the outsider looking in on South Africa solely as armchair observer, the moments caught in such black-and-white photographs disclose social attitudes or experiences more fully than they represent the physical conditions of life. It is no slight to the keen artistry of her fictive constructs when the pictures remind us that Gordimer too has seen and has taken note of such moments, not only invented them. This particular photograph seems virtually the genesis of characters like Mehring's neighbors in *The Conservationist*. Yet again we recall that these are not illustrations for her texts so much as they are reminders of her vision. Like this photographer, she perceives the bulging weight of authority, the intimacy of bodies, as expressed within the social delineations of race, gender, class, and even age, the self-gratifying pride of a difficult balancing act requiring both strength and delicacy in the young white girl trying to be an artist on her family's *stoep*, on her toes.

To grasp how the continuing interaction with African society and its political realities shapes the attitudes and behavior of Gordimer's main characters, we will consider more closely *A World of Strangers*. Though an early work and not one of the author's masterpieces, it affords a clear model of how she delineates significant stages in her characters' development of self-knowledge and therefore identity within an African context.

A World of Strangers begins where its predecessor ended; at the conclusion of *The Lying Days*, the main character, Helen Shaw, is beginning a journey away from South Africa, though with the promise that she will return. Helen's story has comprised a series of thwarted or disappointing attempts at commitments to lovers, friends, causes, and career; juxtaposed against that is the motif of separation from family and the correlative attempt to differentiate and construct an idea of one's self. The National party victory in the 1948 election that put into power a predominantly Afrikaner white-supremacist government resulted in the passage of racist legislation that invaded even the supposedly private domain of white people like Helen. Through such measures as the Prohibition of Mixed Marriages Act and the Immorality Act, whose vicious enforcement the book recounts, Helen comprehends that her own life happens during a particular time in history, within a certain place in the world. Making a commitment to Africa even as she leaves, Helen seems to accept that she is bound by lived experience to the full South Africa, with all of its moods, complexity, cultural diversity, richness, and brutality. She understands that in so doing she has also "accepted disillusion as a beginning rather than an end" (*LD*, 367).

Yet it is one thing to say that in the voice of the emotion-filled voyager, choosing at the last moment to declare that emigration will simply be a vacation. It is a different matter to return from abroad, to look critically with an outsider's eye. It is a different matter still to make a commitment to live within that environment, in whatever ways that one can make such a commitment, while seeing what is there in that place, knowing that one has been elsewhere and could still choose to be elsewhere.

Considered in conventional narrative terms, where we expect a plot in which something identifiable happens to the main character other than simply the acquisition of experience, *A World of Strangers*, though interesting, has very little in the way of a story to tell. Rather, one might say that it has several embryonic stories, none of which develops a full conclusion. Aside from Gordimer's own admission that she had to learn narrative skill as she went on, a reason for the lack of development is that Toby, the narrator, remains an outsider, dwelling and working in South Africa, observing social groups and interacting with various individuals but not living a life of continuing commitment to them. If this is a marginalized position, it is also a privileged position from which to observe and comment on what he sees without being implicated in all of the ramifications and consequences: He is simply a white in South Africa, not a white African.

The narrator's sense of not being at home there is not accidental. Still, for an odd South African reason, he does not feel alienated either; the place itself seems to make for estrangement. Toby soon notes among the inhabitants "an unexpressed desire to dissociate themselves from their milieu" (*WS*, 68). This desire encompasses a wide range of symptoms, from the superficial to the deep, among whites and nonwhites. Included in the superficial is the way a new spot becomes trendily popular, especially if the customers "can pretend they're somewhere else. . . . Anyway, it does give one the illusion one's in a civilized country." This psychosocial theme is repeated in the Tudor motif of the Stratford Bar, where "Henry VIII in a muffin hat . . . stared at a gilt plaster lion that was the symbol of a South African brewery" (WS, 74), and at the lavish party where the pretentious hostess exclaims of her new purchase, a dreadful Courbet, "Can you believe it? I found it here, in Johannesburg!" (WS, 62). Among the deeper symptoms is Toby's closest black friend, Steven's, disgust "with black men's troubles," his refusal to become politically involved because to do so means to immerse himself in constant brooding awareness of social injustice (WS, 102).

At the first integrated party Toby attends, a discussion about painting in the South African context raises directly the cultural issue of what art means in South Africa. Toby has already noted that the awed provincial response to Mrs. Alexander's Courbet ("How do you spell the name?") takes place in a room dominated by what he calls "the Table Bay *genre* . . . not a discomforting brush-stroke in any of them" (WS, 62). A disgruntled white man wishes for what he calls "literary painting" to supplant the dominant landscapes: 'They don't know how to deal with man, so they leave him out" or turn the human figure into a merely decorative element, for example, "those nubile Zulu maidens, all boot-polish breasts and flashing teeth." The man's proposed alternative, however, sounds rather like the Victorian narrative genre painting moved half a world under, depicting the privileged white child playing in the garden, watched by the uniformed African maid, with a street gang passing outside; the aesthetic objections to this kitsch clink hollowly in the ineffectual rejoinder that "much abstract painting is . . . the expression of ideas" (WS, 87). Later, Toby's friend Sam, a composer, collaborates with a white man on an alleged opera that is supposed to be a fusion of two cultures but actually turns out as "a white man's idea of what a black man would write, and a black man's idea of what a white man would expect him to write" (WS, 212). Sam's black friends believe his artistry has been exploited by a white hack. Toby, who recognizes the work is a failure, agrees that Sam is a superior artist to his collaborator; nonetheless, he is also convinced that without the white's involvement, Sam could not have learned the necessary stagecraft, which South Africa racial laws had previously closed to him.

In this setting art is not neutral or color-blind in its substance or production. If—and this if is not strongly challenged by anyone in the book— the standard for achievement is white and Eurocentric, the way to integrate that into the African context remains problematic. The great distance from Europe may mean that the imports (such as the dim, inferior Courbet) are admired simply because they are foreign, not because they are good. Domestic works are likely to be about, rather than of, Africa, with the landscape or people displayed as picturesque. At the edges of possibility seem to be the self-consciously literary, embodied in an issue-oriented literal-mindedness (like "the novel of miscegenation" or the narrative painting) or else in the abstract, expressing ideas that may seem remote from the pressing immediacies of human needs and crises manifesting themselves amid intolerable circumstances. Stephen Clingman has described this novel as "something of a continuing 'generic' debate with [E. M.] Forster" that includes a challenge to that realism which becomes "essentially complicit with the structure of the reality it represents," a realism somewhat undercut in the book by the author's selective use of symbolic modes.[19]

Toby's idea that Sam can benefit from a collaboration obviously could be expanded to include all other areas of culture and society, including the economic and political. If all standards of achievement are Western or European, then the Africans who have been excluded from mastering these (being denied, for instance, such tools of mastership as administrative or managerial appointments or elective offices) have much to learn from apprenticeship or power sharing with the whites, who have had such experience. In reply to Steven's haughty denial that the white coauthor can teach Sam (who has never been to a theater) anything about making an opera, Toby rebuts him: "Don't be a damn fool. Anybody can teach him something. Anybody who's been able to see plays and hear operas" (WS, 214). Clingman points out that in the 1950s the thrust of the freedom movement in South Africa was toward "reform within a given structure of South African reality"—not revolution but integration of blacks into an existing system and nonconfrontational, peaceful protest for civil rights.[20] Even the use of symbolic literary techniques to illuminate the grotesqueries of apartheid, Clingman suggests, implies that effecting change is simply a matter of awakening consciousnesses, which presumably would lead whites to see blacks as individuals, as human as they themselves are, and therefore to deal with them on an equal basis, giving a helping hand as need would demand. Limited and ultimately inconsequential as that is in the political sphere, within the context of A World of Strangers it would seem to offer the hope of personal advancement by opening insights and the hope that there might be a place for strangers to meet.

Toby observes that Cecil, Toby's casually racist lover, and Steven are like one another, "people who had not found commitment" and so enjoy the "strange freedom . . . of the loose end." Toby recognizes that he too had felt this in his native country, aloof from his class privilege yet also detached by his irony and skepticism from the familial iconoclastic liberal passion. Consequently, he now feels "curiously at home, a stranger among people who were strangers to each other" (WS, 168). As an alien, Toby fits (without quite fitting in) different worlds of South African life, bound together for us as readers only by his presence. They rarely overlap. Only in this sort of context does it seem understandable that his best friend and his lover cannot know one another. He is not the mediator among these spheres, merely a participant and observer.

Early in the book Toby rather snidely alludes to "the miscegenation novel now as regular a South African export as gold or fruit" (WS, 46). His own story is not such a tale, but one can sense the potential in both directions, if his ease around black men were to lead him (in defiance of the Immorality Act) to a black lover, or if Cecil were either daring or unbigoted enough to perceive what he himself does about her and his closest black friend, Steven: "Often I thought how well he and Cecil would have got on together, if they could have known each other. Their flaring enthusiasms, their unchannelled energy, their obstinately passionate aimlessness—each would have matched, out-topped the other" (WS, 205). As it stands, even friendship is impossible between the two, except if one reduces the potential friendship to merely miscegenation or conceives of—gives birth to—a *lusus naturae*, a sport of nature. That would have to wait for Hillela in a later novel.

It proves impossible for Steven truly to set race aside, despite his desire to do so, because it is a fact defining the conditions of his existence; yet it is that desire and his determination to live according to it that attract Toby to him and make their relationship possible for both parties. Steven is not the South African black likely to be seen by Toby's activist family back in England, "earnest, bespectacled. . . . who would bore me and bring to the surface ponderous emotions of self-righteousness and guilt . . . a cipher" (WS, 113). As an individual, he can become Toby's friend. The closely detailed social circumstances under which that friendship is lived out, however, are not within Steven's or Toby's power to shape individualistically.

At first, this book seems to be a novel of manners, with its tone set by the narrator's posturing opening: "I hate the faces of peasants" (WS, 7). The well-educated young Englishman aboard the ship that has just docked at its first African port verbally sketches the native scenes and some of his fellow passengers and entertains a flirtation with a married older woman; the gestures of genre suggest perhaps Evelyn Waugh. Indeed, Toby shows himself to be a self-conscious and literary fellow, appropriately enough for a publishing executive who comes of a pedigreed liberal family and has taken an Oxford degree. He is the sort of person who describes his features as "straight out of Dickens and nowhere else" (WS, 10) and will later remark that another character admirably untroubled by moral equivocations or presumptions "reduced life to the narrative" (WS, 244). It soon appears that all his shipmates old enough to do so are themselves posturing, like the consul and his family who "used each other's names all the time, like people in a play" (*WS*, 10), or Stella, the "Byronic" Italophile whose Italy is that of "those young girls in Forster's early novels" rather than that of "Moravia and the realist films" (*WS*, 15). Furthermore, there is the woman who exclaims that the sight of the Mombassa coast is "exactly like something out of Somerset Maugham" (*WS*, 8) but becomes ill the closer she gets to Rhodesia and her farming husband, who supports her frequent and extended continental jaunts.

Toby's grasp of his fellow passengers' escapism, although couched in literary terms, reveals the analytic mind below the superficialities. He perceives in others, as in himself, the capacities for mythologizing. Even he experiences his first physical immersion into the continent (at Nyali Beach, Mombassa) as a transformation, though the eye that hates the faces of peasants will not make the mistakes of the one who refuses to see her Italy through the eyes of Moravia or the realist filmmakers. Toby explains: "I seemed to feel an actual physical melting, as if some component of my blood that had remained insoluble for twenty-six years of English climate had suddenly, wonderfully, dissolved into free-flowing. I gazed in lazy physical joy at the lovely smooth-patterned boles of the coconut palms, waving their far-off bouquets above our heads. . . . The last jagged crystal in my English blood melted away" (*WS*, 14–15). With critical awareness of what experience betokens, he also records the sensibilities at work during a shipboard party that is not merely an entertaining experience but a sort of rite marking off their circle of merriment from those who are not privileged to be included, although they are unable not to notice. The reach for anthropological significance is perhaps somewhat abrupt and forced, and the episode takes on too much symbolic meaning too quickly. But Toby is young, after all, and his social psychology is nonetheless accurate and self-critical, as this passage indicates: "How ridiculously much these trivial things matter in hotels and ships, how they reproduce in miniature the whole human situation, the haves and have-nots, the chosen and the rejected, the prestige of the successful fight for the female, the singling out of their leader by the herd! . . . I was surprised and a little inclined to sneer at myself to find that I enjoyed the warm feeling of being one of the group, of belonging" (*WS*, 23–24). Toby's and Gordimer's honesty about that feeling illuminate his willingness to spend time with the rich and pampered, although he himself is not hedonistic and seems to have few needs or desires for wealth, culinary delights, or physical comfort. Importantly, it is a willingness more than a desire or need. He is always clear that these are not the people he chooses for friendship. The differences are marked for him in the ways they implicitly define the terms of their lives. "They thought of courage in terms of gallantry, spirit in terms of gameness; in the long run, I supposed my mother's and my father's definitions were my own, I could really only think of these things in terms of political imprisonment and the revolt of the intellect" (*WS*, 243–44). "In the long run": In the short term, he is one of those border characters on the margins between two cultures, not quite at home with either, and he has plenty of company there.

Virginia Woolf claimed that being able to support herself had meant far more to her than getting voting rights. That notion seems seconded by Sam when he provides Toby, near the end of the novel, with his explanation of "what it's like to be a black man," a matter not of skin color but of economic obligations to an extended family living below subsistence level. As he explains, "If you've got a decent job with decent money it can't do you much good, because it's got to spread so far. . . . You can't ever get out of debt while there's one member of the family who has to pay a fine or get sick and go to the hospital" (*WS*, 255). This network of bonds is one of the burdens from which Steven has tried to escape, using his considerable intelligence and ingenuity along with "his vitality and resource and time" (*WS*, 204), evading the laws and restrictions hemming him in along with other blacks. Cecil, so much like him, poor and with a child to support, has also struggled her way around financial obligations, but the young white woman will be more successful than the young black man, who finally loses his life fleeing those arbitrary white laws. She explains that her fiancée wants her to get a white nurse for her son so "I can be quite free." Toby recognizes that with a white surrogate available, "there was no need at all for her to be his mother" (*WS*, 262). Cecil can escape both poverty and a familial bond much closer and more finite than those extensive ones to which Sam feels morally bound.

Here Gordimer notes a gulf of possibility between all blacks and even an impoverished white woman. She also reveals the common ground of shared perceptions about their own lives that apartheid keeps screened from poor whites. In an earlier scene, Toby and Cecil discovered a black servant from her building howling and sobbing in a drug-induced frenzy, "his Christmas," as an onlooker explains (*WS*, 200). The phrase sticks with Cecil and below the conscious level triggers an end-of-the-year reflection on her life that sounds very much like what Sam or Steven might say about their lives except that they have learned to live within narrower limits of expectations and prospects. Her protest, made in circumstances far more comfortable than theirs, is nonetheless the frustrated cry of disappointed expectations for bourgeois comforts and a life of personal satisfaction: "What have I got to show? Twenty-nine. Not enough money to live decently. What on earth can I do with myself?" (*WS*, 202). That her language bears the tones of authenticity may owe something to the fact that at twenty-nine Gordimer had also been a poor single mother with a young child (though that was also when her first book was published abroad). During Cecil's complaint Toby hears for the first time the traces of a South African accent "beneath the carefully acquired upper-class English stereotype of her voice," as she longs for money, for a more sophisticated culture far away in Europe, for the freedoms of middle-class success and personal autonomy, for independence from her child. She does not recognize any affinity between blacks and herself as being dependent on a class or category of people who are privileged with the independence, wealth, and power that she cannot herself claim. Though the critical (but not self-critical) appraisal of her life is generated by the black man's desperate attempt at oblivion, and she seems to join in his bitter desperation, sardonically echoing "His Christmas!," the experience leads her only partway toward sociopolitical awareness. She is prepared to blame it on the country but does not conclude that she and the black man share causes. What she resents is being afflicted with "a thing like that on your doorstep. . . . How can you live with savages around you!" (WS, 202). No wonder she will be so clearly baffled that Toby allows "natives" to visit him in his apartment (WS, 262).

The racial theme of the novel is so important that one is inclined to overlook the other motifs to which it is connected. For the book is also about friendships and family ties, the influence of upbringing, and the dissatisfactions of what a later Gordimer novel will call, using a borrowed phrase, "the late bourgeois world." Toby is aware of the division between the racial and the personal, although without any way of resolving it by bridging or prioritizing it. He remarks, for instance, regarding the boasts (true or invented) about sexual relations with white women from Steven and every other even meagerly successful black man, "I suppose that in the country I was living in, in the city I was living in, such tales were sensational, anarchic, and meant far more; but I must say that to me, as a stranger and an outsider, they were simply part of the old sex myth I have mentioned before—the wistful projection of joy not to be had at home" (WS, 193). As expressed in the concluding phrase, this phenomenon is not confined to sex, is not even really about sex, but is found as well in the xenophilia of Stella Turgell and in Cecil and Steven, as well as in the ignorant enthusiasm for foreign art, no matter its quality. We may even hear the suggestion, more fully developed in later novels, that what seems to be a matter of sex is really a matter of liberty and territoriality.

Behind Toby, we remember, sits a South African white female writer, registering through his words the political interpretation of these tales (the popular culture version of miscegenation novels, which she has refused to write here), the personal understanding that they are not always literally true but still signify something true, and the consciousness that such white or black fantasies are not confined to the particular conditions of her country but attest to restless, fantasy-inducing emotional dissatisfaction with the conditions of life. The language Gordimer gives to Toby indicates, however, a critical split in perception between the public and private that seems unbridgeable: The tales are on the one hand "anarchic" and on the other hand "simply part of the old sex myth."

In the private world evoked by the novel, friendships bridge racial divisions, even though that means that Toby escapes being isolated on an island by himself through separate metaphorical bridges of friendship, some leading to the region of the whites, some to the region of the blacks. In that world he can also afford the luxury of rebelling against his parents' and uncle's activism, wanting to associate with those who "amuse" him, while ignoring "the abstractions of race and politics," allowing himself to think, "And to hell with you all!" (WS, 36). There is no question, however, that it is exactly the sort of upbringing he has had that allows him to be dissatisfied with the posh, pampered life around the Alexanders' pool, that it makes it possible for him rather than them to find those "amusing" people of other races and to share drinks, meals, and occasionally a roof with Steven or Sam. Toby's rebellion turns out to be against means, not convictions. If he shuns political activism and refuses to judge Steven negatively for his lack of political commitment, we may ascribe that to the oppressive weight of a family in which Toby's mother's bathtub reading consists of piles of political pamphlets about Africa in transition and in which the dinner guests were likely to be journalists and clergy "who had been to shake a Christian fist in the face of the godless white oppressors in South Africa" (WS, 35). Again it is useful to recall the authorial angle of vision behind the narrative, to suspect that through Toby, Gordimer herself may have registered impatience with the consuming mental demands of political commitment and its resulting abstractions. Also criticized here are the smug condemnations of South African whites by self-righteous Caucasians who have been divinely chosen to reside elsewhere, counterparts to the others advocating removing apartheid through a gradualism that knows no calendar and acknowledges no suffering.

We realize that the absence of plot development can be seen not simply as a literary phenomenon but as a reflection of political realities. Indeed, the final scene of the novel may carry with it a deeper irony or ambiguity. Toby is free to leave South Africa, and Gordimer's second novel ends like the first, with the main character leaving the country while promising to return. Toby, however, promises only a visit, and even this is suspect. In a way he may be seen as a surrogate for white liberals, even native-born South African white liberals for whom emigration is always possible, and it is to them, not just to the English-born Toby Hood, that the black character Sam may be speaking in questioning how steadfast that friendship and those commitments are. "Who knows with you people, Toby, man?" (*WS*, 266). The book, which began with the voyage taking Toby to Africa (by ship, just as the first whites arrived), leaves us with uncertainty as to whether Toby will return, and if so, to what and to whom. His strongest relationships—to the now-dead Steven, whose attempt to make a separate racial peace for himself ends when he is killed in a crash following a police raid on an illegal black township shebeen, to his girlfriend, Cecil, who is about to make her way out of poverty and obligations by marrying a wealthy and alcoholic social celebrity, to the imprisoned political activist Anna Louw—have ended, leaving only the tie to Sam, for whose child's christening Toby pledges to return. This is Toby's pledge of loyal affection to a new Africa, emerging some time beyond the novel.

Gordimer has said, apropos of the ending of *The Conservationist*, that "the only beautiful, politically valid slogan" she knows of is, "Mayibuye": "Come back, Africa."[21] The frequency with which her characters, throughout her career, leave, come back, flee into exile, or are in prison at the end implies how tension-laden the attachments to home, to Africa, are. But so are all close attachments, within which we make lives of sensual experience, attempt to communicate with one another, fail and are failed through secrets and deceptions, and dwell inside our anxieties about home and family relations. We live, her works suggest, perplexed by strangeness to one another and ourselves, seeking our native land, our home.

CHAPTER THREE

KNOWING THROUGH
THE BODY

"What made me become a writer was, first of all, sensuous experience."[1] Gordimer's remark implies more than it says. Deflecting the frequent tendency to take her work as socio-political history while confessing the degree to which a writer is driven by love of the stuff of living, it also calls to mind the extent to which this writer's work in particular is suffused with the sensuous. To say this about it is almost to state a commonplace, though a paradoxical commonplace, for her books are also tagged as absorbed by political ideas, "somewhat tendentious," in Diane Johnson's phrase.[2] Still, to others, Gordimer's work bespeaks, as Judith Thurman has written, "lyrical eroticism," which does not simply nestle in the text but stimulates "small, expertly focused, pleasurable sensations that relax a reader, and . . . flashes of mystery that draw one into a story."[3] The watchmaker's daughter, the young woman who loved dancing ("the pleasure, the release, of using the body in this way"), developed into a writer attentive to details, responsive to the link between bodily experience and understanding.[4] Goethe's metaphor is one that she often cites, and fittingly so for its description of creativity as a physical involvement with the stuff of life. As Gordimer once paraphrased it, "You thrust your hand deep into the life around you, and whatever you bring up will have something of the truth there. But you've got to thrust deep into it."[5] No wonder she was attracted to Barthes's definition of writing as the writer's "essential gesture." Not just "statement" or "business"—*gesture.*[6]

That physicality gives particular energy to Gordimer's descriptions, just as it complements her attention to sexuality. It may emerge, through sight and sound, even when she focuses attention on something fearsome, such as the dragon-toothed razor wire ringing the top of a high wall that protects a white home: "The sunlight flashed and slashed, off the serrations, the cornice of razor thorns encircled the home, shining" (J, 30). Yet even in her accounts of travels through Africa, those descriptions are never hovered over for their own sake. The author seems more a descriptive writer than a writer of descriptions. See how the quick-sketch details jot a landscape (here, that of Pondoland in the Transkei) onto a notepad: "Looking from mountains on to mountains: dark ploughed land cast like nets, there; velour of light on contours of rose, blond and bronze grasses. Where the grass has been burnt, coal-blue shapes; where the first rains have fallen on these, stains of livid growth spread as the shadow of the clouds do."[7] The immediacy of her "there," like an interjection; the texture carried by "velour"; the vegetable, human, and mineral undertones of the three adjectives for the grasses ("rose, blond and bronze") turn description into sensation. If one pauses to ask whether there is a method or moral to the description, the answer is probably yes, but not in the way of a Spenserian landscape. The energy is not unlike what we might associate with D. H. Lawrence, without his obsessiveness or his metaphysics. What we see here is a surface, but it is alive, vital, and varying. We sense energy flowing to that surface from inside and know that there truly is more here than the eye records.

The same can be said for Gordimer's descriptions of people she sees on her travels, such as this "queen" observed in Botswana, "standing tall and a little apart, with a turned-down amusement on her sardonic mouth. She perversely wore an old striped towel half-concealing her kilt of handmade ostrich shell beads and hide thongs, and her long legs with their calf-bracelets of copper and hide, but her slender, male youth's shoulders and the flat breasts her body seemed almost to disdain, the assertion of her long neck and shaven head, resolved all aesthetic contradictions."[8] It is all surface, and not just because this traveler cannot know anything else; however, the surface becomes its own magnificence, carries with it—and here is the foundation of the technique—its own declaration of independence. In this instance that is also the independence of the female subject, the androgyne, not sexless but seeming to fulfill elements of both sexes in the vicinity of two hills, really named Male and Female, which occupy the center of her people's creation myth. Actually, "The prow of Male hill rose behind her" is ambiguous: Is it like the rock-painting figures Gordimer has just seen in these hills, "dancing men with innocent erect penises that have no erotic significance and persist as a permanent feature of Bushman anatomy, even today"?[9] The contradictions the woman comprises she holds together herself, despite their variety, by personal aplomb.

The connotations of such a description need to be considered; for the woman, looked at, studied, anatomized, does seem to become objectified. We might be faced with an image of remote ethnic exotica from an old travelogue or a *National Geographic*. Is she not like a landscape, except for the gender markers, which oddly defeminize her? She is admired, but she is rather like a curio, this black African whom the white African studies, this woman whose gender-aware depiction almost threatens to become an appraisal. The description is almost like the decorative pictures scornfully referred to in *A World of Strangers* showing "those nubile Zulu maidens."

But not quite. In implying manner, control and volition—through terms such as *disdain, assertion,* and *resolved all aesthetic contradictions*— the author acknowledges that her almost-mythic subject ("she of the Mbukushu") lives on a level of consciousness, of self-possession, beyond that familiar creature of colonial projection, the unaware and innocently simple primitive who cannot resist childlike gewgaws. Behind that "sardonic smile" lies knowledgeable sophistication of its own fashion, less the Mona Lisa's smile than the artist's, resolving "all aesthetic contradictions."

The social and political implications of so revising the image should not be underestimated. This woman emerges as a natural leader, designated as such by manner and by her sense of herself; she is not merely another smiling tribeswoman but an individual, engrossing in her own right, interesting as a human being. One cannot doubt her competence or capacity— if given the means to effect it—of governing her own life or those of others, sensitive to those "contradictions" that make life rich and interesting. Perhaps in the Western world at large, where *variety* seems only an advertising slogan and *resolving aesthetic contradictions* merely a fashion statement, this anatomy of the seen turns her into the picturesque. From a South African angle of vision, it brings forth a unique, powerful, richly complex, and sophisticated individual who is female, African, black.

Sensual experience's strong grip is evinced throughout Gordimer's work as a primary means of experiential knowledge. So the colored schoolteacher in *My Son's Story* discovers, in gazing freshly at the white woman he loves, that he is learning about art and perception as well as sexuality and a male attitude toward women.

> Seeing Hannah's fair eyelashes catching the morning sun and the shine of the few little cat's whiskers that were revealed, in this innocent early clarity, at the upper corners of her mouth, he was seeing the whole of her; he understood why, in the reproductions of paintings he had puzzled over in the days of his self-education, Picasso represented frontally all the features of a woman, head, breasts, eyes, vagina, nose, buttocks, mouth—as if all were always present even to the casual glance. What would he have known, without Hannah! (*MSS*, 102)

The jogger in "Keeping Fit," who flees a black gang pursuing a youth, realizes as he jogs home safely, "Suddenly, this was sensational" (*J*, 238). In other words, this was what the victim's sensation of an attack would be. The news reports have been turned into experience, though for him, still vicarious.

Oddly, food and drink are rarely significant sensations in themselves: Although food and occasionally even a specific dish may be mentioned, it is hard to think of a character in Gordimer's work who is a glutton, much less a gourmet who really comments with enjoyment on the taste of what he or she consumes. Such restraint seems appropriate in a social context in which so many lack even sufficient food for survival; sights and sounds are at least more democratically available.

Rather than conveying the gourmet's appreciation of tastes, the author registers the social implications of sharing or not sharing meals, serving or being served; again, this is appropriate in a country where race has determined where one eats, or what, and (often) whether, as well as with whom. Vusi and Eddie in "Something out There" ask to be fed decent meat rather than sausages by their confederate, and Hillela's social movements could be traced by such culinary markers as the fish cooked in green coconut milk or the cornmeal and cabbage. The white leftist in a more recent story ("Comrades") who invites a group of young black activists to her home after a conference helps her maid arrange a meal for them and "suddenly did not want them to see that the maid waited on her. She herself carried the heavy tray into the dining-room," where she attempted to be sociable to these hungry young men for whom her conversation is merely peripheral to the assuaging of their genuine hunger, young men unsure of the rules of behavior "in this room which is a room where apparently people only eat, do not cook, do not sleep" (*J*, 94–95). Their enjoyment of the bowl of fruit, an afterthought she has produced to round out her skimpy provisions, reveals the austere conditions of their own lives. In *A World of Strangers*, Toby's lover, Cecil, frankly expresses her puzzlement at learning of Toby's socializing with black friends: "You mean you can actually sit down to dinner with them and it doesn't seem any different to you?" (*WS*, 263).

Gordimer, speaking of the black servant who worked for her family for thirty-seven years, recalled, "there were cups in the kitchen, and I remember being told, 'No, don't drink out of that,' because those were the cups that Lettie and her friends drank out of. And it didn't occur to me, in my innocence, you know—'What is she going to give me? What was there on the rim of the cup that I didn't get when I sat cuddled up to her on her lap?' This question of the cups remained with me very strongly . . . so there was this physical feeling."[10] During a career that has offered some depth of recompense for Lettie Mbelo's nurturance, the forcefulness of "physical feeling" persists through the writer's sensitivity to physical details ("on the rim of the cup"), as well as through her appraisal of what the physical means to human understanding and social interaction. When Rosa Burger experiences the great division separating the two groups attending Flora's women's rights meeting, she does so through olfactory awareness of a class (not race) division, delineated with a precise distinction between "ladies" and "women," implicitly repudiating the racist belief that "blacks" smell "different" from "whites" by recalling that smells emerge in a social and economic context, as Rosa experiences, "The cosmetic perfumes of the middle-class white and black ladies and the coal-smoke and vaginal odours of old poor black women" (BD, 204). Similarly, the horror of her social displacement comes most strongly to Maureen Smales out in the bush when "for the first time in her life she found that she smelled bad between her legs and . . . disgustedly scrubbed at the smooth lining of her vagina and the unseen knot of her anus in the scum and suds" (JP, 9). The niceties of nutrition, sanitation, and scents become the means to mark, divide, evaluate. The mother in "My Father Leaves Home" expresses this when she physically and verbally scorns her husband, an immigrant from Eastern Europe:

> when he got into bed beside his wife in the dark after those Masonic gatherings she turned away, with her potent disgust, from the smell of whisky on him. . . . She must have read something somewhere that served as a taunt: you slept like animals round a stove, stinking of garlic, you bathed once a week. The children knew how low it was to be unwashed. And whipped into anger, he knew the lowest category of all in her country, this country. *"You speak to me as if I was a kaffir."* (J, 64)

Having learned the most contemptuous South African epithet for a black person in "her country" (which is also "this," but not quite his, country), he recognizes what is implied in her language of disdain, the vocabulary of sensory revulsion.

This is why personification and anthropomorphic imagery become something beyond literary devices in Gordimer's writing. They bespeak the living but usually unperceived existence of connecting tissue within the substance of life. Here, for instance, the aging, genteel Clara Hansen stepping into the evening air to track down her aged but still-philandering husband encounters an airy presence at once vaporously elusive and caressing: "It laid itself lightly, moistly, muffledly against her face; she breathed it and it was not there, so that, breathing it, you would wonder how you lived on something so meltingly substanceless. . . . She did not feel it blowing but it blew, sculpting the silk of her coat against her thighs and legs, spreading the escaped tendrils of her hair against her hat.[11] At times the human and vegetable, animate and inanimate are so woven together, so thoroughly intertwined through Gordimer's prose, that tenor and vehicle seem indistinguishable. One loses track of which is the simile of which in these passages from various works. Notice how elaborately she evokes a house in the first quotation through a simile that seems to become an extended metaphor yet undermines the image through the declaration that "there was no house." In the second and third passages the plant and the fetish similarly emerge as visually compelling tropes that do not illustrate so much as embody the experience they seem to describe.

> The long yelping of the jackals prowled the sky without, like the wind about a house; there was no house, but the sounds beyond the light his fire tremblingly inflated into the dark—that jumble of meaningless voices, crying babies, coughs and hawking—had built walls to enclose and a roof to shelter. ("The Bridegroom," *Sel*, 181)

> It seemed to burst through her mouth in a sudden irresistible germination, the way a creeper shoots and uncurls into leaf and stem in one of those films which telescope plant growth into the space of a few terrifyingly vital seconds. ("Happy Event," *Sel*, 107)

> The laws made of skin and hair fill the statute books in Pretoria; their gaudy savagery paints the bodies of Afrikaner diplomats under three-piece American suits and Italian silk ties. The stinking fetish made of contrasting bits of skin and hair, the scalping of millions of lives, dangles on the cross in place of Christ (*SN*, 179).

In these quotations the natural and social worlds are like one another in a special way. They are not simply analogous by virtue of some attribute; they are part of the world's habitations and thus suggest the unity of all experience. Biological and political become one. That truth, so complexly unfolded in the two most recent novels (*A Sport of Nature* and *My Son's Story*), is richly articulated in a particular moment in the latter book. At a graveside political rally in a black cemetery, members of different races join in a brief time of seamless unity intensified by the ominous presence of the heavily armed police and soldiers marshalled on an overlooking hillside, from which (as we fear) they will shortly launch a murderous charge. "A woman's French perfume and the sweat of a drunk merged as if one breath came from them. And yet it was not alarming for the whites; in fact, an old fear of closeness, of the odours and heat of other flesh, was gone. One ultimate body of bodies was inhaling and exhaling in the single diastole and systole, and above was the freedom of the great open afternoon sky" (*MSS*, 110). To the extent that any metaphysical presence hangs over this graveyard scene, it is the presence of freedom itself, the one deity that matters. Beneath that presence, in the flesh that is not grass, live the lungs and heart of one organism, undifferentiated humanity itself, so blended as to "resolve all aesthetic contradictions"; and color—as if allowed to become an irrelevance—evaporates.

Gordimer's appreciation of the physical sources of comprehension allows her incisive assessment of the likely genesis of Sarah Gertrude Millin's bigotry. Gordimer perceives that, "the metaphor of the 'taint' of colour as 'a catching disease' (used by the heroine of one of her books) is perhaps the life-long metaphor for the fear of the drunkenness and brutal sexual behaviour that were the only experience outside her 'white' home she had as a child. Black was frightening; sex was black *and* frightening; both seemed to her a threat to wholeness, health—whiteness." [12] Millin's sexual repression, which Gordimer also identifies in the other writer's insomnia, is thus linked to racial anxiety, the two presumably fused in early childhood spent around the Kimberley diamond workers. Gordimer, also raised in a mining town, understands the power of those instilled myths and fantasies. In *Occasion for Loving* (1963), her third novel, the liberal Jessie explains to a black male friend the racial sexual patterns inculcated early in her, which dwelt on, "The black man that I must never be left alone with in the house. . . . I used to feel, at night, when I turned my back to the dark passage . . . that someone was coming up behind me. Who was it, do you think? And how many more little white girls are there for whom the very first man was a black man? The very first man, the man of the sex fantasies" (*OL*, 267). [13] Gordimer denounces Millin's failure to go beyond this image, as both she herself and her character Jessie have done, by seeking out "relationships with blacks who were on her own intellectual level" or at least feeling "empathy with, indignation at the suffering she had witnessed," instead of "only condemnation" of the sufferers. Empathy and indignation lead the later writer to situating antipathy and fear within a social context, moving beyond childhood acceptance of what is to ask such inconvenient but transforming questions about the life of her family's servant as, "'Why didn't this woman have a bath[room]?' You know, you'd be afraid of her because she's supposed not to be clean, but you don't provide the means of her keeping herself comfortably clean. Of course, she *was* clean, but there it was. . . . It's amazing how quickly you can change as an adult." [14] One of life's mysteries is how that change comes about inside, why some people and not others take that next step. Gordimer's response is that society or circumstance do not explain all, that character and psychology are also accountable, as in Millin's case, when "a woman with a writer's insight" also bears "a repugnant and twisted personality."[15]

Of course, to say this is to explain nothing—or even worse, to leave us torn between condemnation and exculpation, both loathing and pitying "this brilliant woman" and "remarkably good writer" trapped in a personality that eventually "destroyed the writer . . . her crop stuffed with colour prejudice." But the key to the other writer's failure of self-examination is, for Gordimer, alienation from the physical. A politically active character in the story "Something for the Time Being" considers that her husband, a business executive, "might achieve in five minutes" more valuable results than she does through all of her protest activities, though "she knew that she had to see, touch and talk to people in order to care about them, that's all there was to it" (*Sel*, 221). We grasp vindication of her self-apologetic, even self-dismissive outlook when she realizes the true significance of her husband's revelation that he required the formerly jailed black activist, whom he risked hiring, to take off his ANC pin: "Anything except his self-respect. . . . You'll let him have anything except the one thing worth giving" (*SEL*, 226).

Let us consider, by way of contrast, two episodes from a fairly early story, "The Smell of Death and Flowers," in which physical experience affords crucial education. A young white woman (twenty-two, about the age at which the author herself had gone to university and been politically awakened) draws into political commitment at a multiracial party in Johannesburg where she finds herself dancing, for the first time, with a black African, an experience important for her precisely because the sensation itself surprises her by having so little meaning. (The momentous import of such contact for a white South African woman may be suggested by the fact that the author herself could recall in a 1986 interview "the first black man I ever danced with," around 1949.[16])

> She would not let herself formulate the words in her brain: I am dancing with a black man. But she allowed herself to question, with the careful detachment of scientific inquiry, quietly inside herself: "Do I feel anything? . . . Is this exactly how I always dance?" she asked herself closely. "Do I always hold my back exactly like this, do I relax just this much, hold myself in reserve to just this degree?"
> She found she was dancing as she always danced.
> *I feel nothing*, she thought. *I feel nothing*. (*Sel*, 127)

Devoid of eroticism, devoid of titillation or apprehension, the event simply becomes a casual encounter between two individuals. The next point at which she is aware that "I feel *nothing*" is the moment when the political commitment she made at that party becomes real, and she is placed under arrest for entering a township prohibited to whites. This void of feeling, however, is superseded immediately when, meeting the gaze of a small group of black people ("two men, a small boy and a woman") looking at her, she sees herself through their eyes and, even more importantly, goes beyond sight to empathy: "And she felt, suddenly, not *nothing*, but what they were feeling at the sight of her, a white girl, taken—incomprehensibly, as they themselves were used to being taken—under the force of white men's wills, which dispensed and withdrew life, imprisoned and set free, fed or starved, like God himself" (144). In this moment the identification between the two groups who are not white men—the white woman, the female and male Africans of different ages—becomes as complete as it ever can be in such a country, and while the emphasis seems to be on the sight of her, what seems more important is that she believes she feels what it is to be them, watching this familiar exercise of power "incomprehensibly," because the target is so unfamiliar a victim, but in a way to which they are all accustomed, "taken—under the force of white men's wills." This language suggests an ironic inversion of the rape theme alluded to by Jessie, cited above, when she spoke of the carefully induced fear of black men. The interracial dancing (presumed provocative in mid-1950s South Africa) proves devoid of sexuality or tensions of hierarchy; the true danger, to "her, a white girl," comes from the same source as the danger to the black Africans, the white men who lay claim to all.

Recognizing the mythology of sex and comprehending its sensual power while being able to demythologize and desensualize sex shows what else it can be: an alliance for power or sympathy, an element of barter. So Liz appraises it in *The Late Bourgeois World*, as she thinks to herself about Luke, the black activist who has asked her for a financial favor for the movement: "Oh yes, and it's quite possible he'll make love to me, next time or some time. That's part of the bargain. It's honest, too, like his vanity, his lies, the loans he doesn't pay back: it's all he's got to offer me. . . . Who's to say it shouldn't be called love? You can't do more than give what you have" (*LBW*, 119). In *A Sport of Nature* Hillela lies in bed with her African husband, comparing skin tones and hair textures—an unavoidable South African obsession, the author indicates. Pregnant, she wonders about the color of their baby. "I love not knowing what it will be. What colour it is, already, here inside me. Our colour." That concept is itself a mystery: "A category that doesn't exist: she would invent it. There are Hotnots and half-castes, two-coffee-one-milk, touch-of-the-tar-brush, pure white, black is beautiful—but a creature made of love, without a label; that's a freak" (*SN*, 179). Not only Hillela but the child of her and Whaila is the sport of nature, the oddity not accountable by natural expectations, and the irony is that each is the most natural-seeming entity in the world, a person who loves without recognizing labels, and a child created out of love, "without a label."

Such an imagined category is uncomfortably confronted with reality. The first is the assassination of her husband, the child's father. The second is the real life lived in the world stripped of romanticism, the world inside the tourist's color photographs. "The real rainbow family stinks. The dried liquid of dysentery streaks the legs of babies and old men and the women smell of their monthly blood. They smell of lack of water. They smell of lack of food. They smell of bodies blown up by the expanding gases of their corpses' innards, lying in the bush in the sun" (SN, 251). Acquainted with parched landscapes and the power of the drill (which she has turned into a metaphor, on more than one occasion, to characterize the writer's work), Gordimer has expressed the objective of writers committed to social reform, "asking of themselves means that will plunge like a drill to release the great primal spout of creativity, drench the censors, cleanse the statute books of their pornography of racist and sexist laws, hose down religious differences, extinguish napalm bombs and flame-throwers, wash away pollution from land, sea and air, and bring out human beings into the occasional summer fount of naked joy." [17] "Herculean" seems more appropriate than "heroic" for this mighty task, while its Whitmanesque or Lawrentian idyllic vision of a new Eden surprisingly links its author with a wellspring of romantic carnal exuberance.

In a detailed, perceptive review of A Sport of Nature, Judith Thurman observes, "The precision and delight with which Gordimer describes Hillela's body—taut cheekbones, full breasts, skin that constantly tingles with intelligence and pleasure—suggest that it is just the kind of place a moralist might choose for her vacation." [18] This almost has it right: almost because Thurman, in treating the book's mythmaking eroticism as an authorial caprice, seems to imply a dichotomy between the force of the author's moral judgment ("her fury," Thurman calls it) and "her lyrical eroticism," both of which the critic terms, admiringly, "shameless." This is to put the wrong traits to Gordimer's moralizing, which (as that prophetic vision of purifying creativity expresses) is meant to be liberating. So Thurman is right in noticing that (among other associations) the heroine's name "suggests the landscape of a woman's body—a body that will prove to be this novel's 'liberated territory.'"

To use that metaphor is to begin suggesting why critics find this book so discomfitting. Diane Johnson wondered, "Is the author mocking, predicting, or merely wishing?" [19] Other reviewers granted no benefits of any doubts, dismissing it as "glib" and suggesting Judith Krantz and Sidney Sheldon as the artistic forerunners. Readers, especially female readers, have been unsettled by other aspects of the work. Why does it celebrate a sexually attractive and accessible but apparently aimless white woman whose rise to prominence in African liberation movements is accomplished by her skill in bedding and unfailingly delighting the right African revolutionaries, an embodiment (literally) of fantasies about interracial relationships and sexual availability? Why is she obsessed, in her first marriage, not only with apparently insatiable sexual hunger for her "obsidian" husband but with an irrepressible and politically irresponsible craving for him "to 'give her'—that was how she put it—another baby at once" (*SN*, 189)? In Thurman's words, "Gordimer has rarely bestowed her affection on a *female* who has so little ethical tension to her character." [20]

Uncertainty extends beyond the heroine's depiction. Why, for instance, are no black women significant in this book? Are we supposed to pass over, with complete equanimity and without irony or criticism, a sentence such as this one, following one of the military victories of her lover, whom she has been providing with both secretarial and sexual support: "When the General sent her out during the mopping-up operations (which included the looting of bars and brothels by some of his long-deprived troops) it was from his stance on this strategic bit of liberated territory that he saw her off in one of his Libyan planes" (*SN*, 287). If we read bitter irony in the conjunction of "liberated territory" with the pitiless phrase "looting of . . . brothels" (the prostitutes thus disposed of like whiskey bottles), against whom is the irony directed, and of what moral or political point is it? If there is no irony, why is there also no empathy? Especially in this context, how can we take, approvingly, the metaphors of phallic orgasm and physical violence that become the celebration of a liberated South Africa at the novel's conclusion, as "Cannons ejaculate from the Castle" and the new flag, emerging like a chrysalis, "is smoothed taut by the fist of the wind" (*SN*, 341)? Are the final images meant to validate a black African male sexuality that has all the appearance of machismo, in a direct rebuff to emasculating laws and customs constructed to suppress African expressions of sexuality and power in South Africa?

The larger question of how one reads this book turns out to be inseparable from the questions of who is doing the reading and where that reader lives, as reviewers have noted in contrasting ways. We can see in the following quotations that the critics (Diane Johnson first, Tom Wilhelmus second) have suspected that the book may read differently outside South Africa than inside, indeed, that it may be politically or spiritually efficacious to (some) South Africans, thereby justifying the aesthetic or formalistic peculiarities or shortcomings to which those of us outside South Africa might have the luxury of objecting:

This final fantasy of a political eventuality so desirable and unlikely must doubtless be reassuring to the South African reader. For others, it calls into question the generic assumptions of the book, the rules by which we must try to understand it.[21]

From the outset, . . . the "art" in *A Sport of Nature* appears deeply compromised by the "life" it attempts to describe. In South Africa life is evil, and a case may be made that conventional novels only nourish that evil. . . . As an essay on the effect of history upon the individual the book seems entirely convincing. Others will complain that it is not a novel and does not produce the same satisfactions that a novel provides. And they will be right. The author herself would lament the fact that the evil in South Africa affords no more pleasing solution.[22]

Both Thurman and Johnson have commented, in their reviews, on Gordimer's authorial coldness toward whites in Africa, even—perhaps especially—the good liberals, an attitude "approaching intolerance" in this book according to the former and to the latter "a certain malice toward white people, especially those of her own camp . . . a kind of objectivity amounting almost to distaste."[23] It is certainly true that, as Johnson notes, Gordimer withholds sympathy from "those of her own camp—English speakers, bourgeois liberals, radicals, Jewish intellectuals." In Gordimer's vision of Africa, these are hardly the people who she believes need patronage; undoubtedly this coldly critical gaze is complemented by a certain austerity of attention characteristic of the author's style throughout her career. Johnson notes that "charm and humor" are not abundant, and "there are no jokes in Gordimer, anywhere."[24] If these are accurate appraisals, they point toward the genesis of the tone and plot in *A Sport of Nature*, the search for a white South African who is an authentic human being fully receptive and available to instinct and experience. A passage in a later book, *My Son's Story*, takes us to an "earlier" historical stage, therefore to a time before such a liberated person can emerge, unconscious of the racial implications of living in the body, unaware of the socially acculturated sense of self that does become a sense of separateness. "The blacks were accustomed to closeness. In queues for transport, for work permits, for housing allocation, for all the stamped paper that authorized their lives; loaded into overcrowded trains and buses to take them back and forth across the veld, fitting a family into one room, they cannot keep the outline of space—another, invisible skin—whites project around themselves, distanced from each other in everything but sexual and parental intimacy" (*MSS*, 110). Once again we find the author catching the corner of a romanticized view of black life (here, the "closeness"), affirming an aspect of truthfulness in

observable experience while delineating the oppression out of which that
has come; her verb *cannot keep* forbids us to take this as an essentialist
conception of black people or a deliberate black preservation of values superior to those of white culture. A white person might lament the personal
and metaphysical costs of people being "distanced from each other," but
South African blacks, Gordimer indicates, have no choice to make. The
closeness perhaps envied (and idealized) by those who have, as July's wife
had been told, a "room to sleep in, another room to eat in, another room
to sit in, a room with books" is, for black people, something to which they
become "accustomed" by the circumstances of their lives (*JP,* 19).

By means of the character of Hillela, Gordimer seems to haul up the
mythic taboos of race and color into clear view to shove them over. Hillela
reveals to us—in fact gives to her first "colored" boyfriend and then to a
succession of black African lovers—the woman of their fantasies. The colored adolescent narrator of the next novel acknowledges the enticement of
the fantasy: "She is blonde, my father's woman. Of course. What else
would she be? How else would he be caught? . . . Of course she is blonde.
The wetdreams I have, a schoolboy who's never slept with a woman, are
blonde. It's an infection brought to us by the laws that have decided what
we are, and what they are—the blonde ones" (*MSS,* 13–14). Through Hillela, Gordimer seems to be positing what a person might be like if freed
from the overlay of repression and the constrictions of separateness. We
have already noted that the author frequently connects sexual with politically revolutionary energy. So often Gordimer's own language for free artistic creativity suggests not merely going "below the surface" but drilling
or chiseling through a hard, intractable layer to get at some deeply covered
truth or to release energy that has been contained under pressure. Romantic freedom, as expressed in the fountain passage above, bursts through
unnatural authoritarian structures laid on top of our common humanity,
which we otherwise could feel and enjoy: In Gordimer's words, "The
brotherhood of man . . . is the only definition of society that has any permanent validity."[25] So the main motivating force for Hillela apparently is
not political conviction, which white liberals like her aunts hold in sufficient measure, but something far less intellectual and more universally
human. Hillela "has never been one to make mistakes when following her
instincts" (*SN,* 195). Appropriately enough, when she must "complete" by
herself the "education" in revolution that she had begun to receive from
Whaila, it is not academic but practical: "She taught herself not the old
theories of ends, but the diplomacy and technicalities of means, that were
immediate. She mastered specifications of guns and missiles and their relative suitability for the conditions under which they would have to be
used" (*SN,* 219). Like the saboteurs in "Something out There," working

for black rights with "the terrible tools that were all they had to work with," Hillela knows as much as she has to, in the way that she has to; for the principle of equality—"the brotherhood of man"—is one that she already understands by the instinct that draws her to her lovers, those whom Thurman calls "men for the woman warrior's delight" (*SOT,* 203).[26] The texts of Leon Trotsky and Frantz Fanon, of Kwameh Nkrumah and Antonio Gramsci, even of Govan Mbeki and Joe Slovo, would offer explanations and justifications that are merely superfluous to her understanding, through the skin and inner sensibilities. She affirms, in her own way, the personal politics of compassion Rosa Burger declared:

> I don't know the ideology.
> It's about suffering.
> How to end suffering. (*BD,* 332)

Anomalous as she may seem, Hillela bears some deep, striking similarity to Gordimer's other heroines. Take, for instance, her attitude toward sex, which is a freer and more joyful version of Rebecca's in *A Guest of Honour.* In that book we meet another woman who takes sex easily through a long series of lovers, moving without premeditation into the role of compassionate and supportive mistress to Bray in the absence of his wife and working in politics though not herself politically motivated. Toward men other than Bray, her sexual receptivity comes from pity, understanding, and indifference: "When they made passes at me—Neil, the others—I saw that they felt they could do it because *to me* they could risk showing that things weren't so good for them, either. I felt sorry for them. I felt what did it matter" (*GH,* 463). With Bray, she proves herself "a woman full of sexual pride," displaying herself to him (in a passage strikingly similar to one in *A Sport of Nature,* 258) before "she reached up under his body and took the whole business, the heavy bunch of sex, in her hands" (*GH,* 238) to enjoy prior to guiding him in. During fellatio in another episode, she takes him past "an intensity that had lain sealed in him all his life. . . . Barrier after barrier was passed, each farthest shore was gained and left behind" (*GH,* 279). Rebecca, in turn, seems to have a more directly committed attitude toward sexual expression than her immediate predecessor, Liz, in *A Late Bourgeois World,* who was willing to take sex as love because that may be all her partners have to give. Liz, in turn, is more politically and socially conscious of the ramifications of her commitments than her predecessor, the sensual Ann of *Occasion for Loving,* who took a black lover without racial consciousness as "man to her woman" and joins easily and skillfully in the black township dances. Another of Gordimer's female characters who experiences freedom the way the author as a young child did, through dancing, Ann "quickly became as good as the best of the black girls; like them, she could dance with her whole body and use muscles that most white women do not know are theirs to command" (*OL*, 94–95). Though a forerunner of Hillela in these regards, Ann does not have Hillela's independence from family or social connections. Consequently, her obliviousness to what she is doing leaves not liberation but wreckage behind.

Hillela's kinship with Rosa Burger (made particularly apposite by the fact that Rosa makes a brief walk-on appearance in the later novel) is even more interesting and complex. The one devoid of a surname and unequivocal family identity (other than a parental legacy of sexual irresponsibility), the other burdened by the surname binding her—"Burger's daughter"—to a tradition of revolutionary involvement, the two young women grow through involvements with others that challenge or even tempt them to withdrawal or action. Rosa, having made her getaway from South Africa, is drawn to the Riviera villa of her father's first wife, a Communist living a comfortable but not lavish semiretirement. The young woman luxuriates in this holiday idyll, which becomes, for her, something like the epic hero's withdrawal into pastoral seclusion (and, like most of those heroes, she does not know that its atemporal languor will suit her only temporarily). "Dissolving in the wine and pleasure of scents, sights and sounds existing only in themselves, associated with nothing and nobody, Rosa Burger's sense of herself was lazily objective. The sea, the softly throbbing blood in her hands lolling from the chair-arms, time as only the sundial of the wall's advancing shadow, all lapped tidelessly without distinction of within or around her" (*BD*, 222). The absence of significant associations permits her to "dissolve," to slip the identity so heavily overdetermined in her native land, so that the sea's pulse, her own, and the solar movement blend seamlessly. Shortly after, she will claim the nymph's image created for her by her hostess, who is also an experienced sensualist.

> A big jar of lilac, scent of peaches furry in a bowl, dim mirrors, feminine bric-a-brac of bottles and brushes, a little screen of ruched taffeta for social intimacies, a long cane chair to read the poetry and elegant magazines in, a large low bed to bring a lover to. It was a room made ready for someone imagined. A girl, a creature whose sense of existence would be in her nose buried in flowers, peach juice running down her chin, face tended at mirrors, mind dreamily diverted, body seeking pleasure. Rosa Burger entered, going forward into possession by that image. (*BD*, 229–30)

The would-be lover (her pastoral swain, who is in fact the well-tended lover of a wealthy woman some years his senior) appears, makes his move when she cuts her toe in the water, with a fully erotic overture dashingly taking it in his mouth, while she thinks,

> ridiculous at the same time as sensual. . . . But it was done with such confidence I understood it as I was meant to.
> As he squatted there before me I saw and felt his head, his tongue as if it were between my legs—he knew it. (*BD*, 240)

She resists him, spotting his technique for what it is, an almost unthinking compulsion to offer himself erotically, but the enveloping physical luxury of southern France and the moral luxury of radicals in retirement—free to analyze and criticize from the comfortable distances in space and time—continue her dissolution. She eventually does take a lover, a leftist French journalist whom she promises to follow to Paris as his mistress, to be set up in a studio or a small hotel, perhaps in anticipation of their spending a year together somewhere in Africa. There are, of course, "a wife and two children, a responsibility assumed long ago by a responsible man," but still, "I live among my wife and children—not with them" (*BD*, 289). As mistress, Rosa would live outside the associations of family, the certainties of public role and class placement. "I really do not know if I want any form of public statement, status, code; such as marriage. There's nothing more private and personal than the life of a mistress, is there?" (*BD*, 304). Living a private life, she can feel free to define herself, to accept Katya's or Bernard's way of imagining her or to make herself someone of her own devising, with her own self-generated commitments: "She's certainly not accountable to the Future, she can go off and do good works in Cameroun or contemplate the unicorn in the tapestry forest" (*BD*, 304).

Such freedom the young Hillela enjoys by being cast out, devoid of familial links that would shape her choices. Later in her life, sent to negotiate with her lover's rebellious son, who is exiled under house arrest and who apparently becomes, in due course, also her lover, Hillela "had no understanding, was free of the patricidal and infanticidal loves between parents and children" (*SN*, 285). She also is offered a comfortable escape from imposed political commitments through the contemplated marriage to a young, adoring American patrician from a long line of liberals, a comfortable and wealthy lover whose familiar brownstone they furnish together and who is intoxicated by her sensual offerings, "as if the bountiful pleasures welled up in her, the more she gave—here, here, Brad—the more she had to give" (*SN*, 258). To Hillela, he offers "certainty. . . . No need to watch out about how to manage. . . . No caution necessary about whom you are seen with. . . . No need to watch for what can be traded . . . in exchange for a stamp on a piece of paper. Once married to a bona fide citizen of a country already existing and not still to be won back, there is full citizenship of the present" (*SN*, 260). That is, the unmarried affiliation for Rosa and the marriage for Hillela would both have the same consequences, permission to live in the present.

The present turns out, for women like these, to be an elusive place. First of all, the past still exists as a continuing reality in their lives, a reality to which they still are attached. For Rosa, the past returns through an inadvertent meeting with "Baasie," the black man who was raised as a child by her parents and who now has claimed the right to redefine his identity and so reinterpret their past in ways that challenge and upset her. Hillela's past lives on in the daughter she bore Whaila, a daughter she named for Nomzamo Winnie Mandela and who is most often alluded to in the novel simply as "the namesake," a talismanic reminder of her links with another time and being.

Second of all, Africa—Africa in revolt—is also part of their present and united with it, in them, through their roots. Rosa returns there to go back to work as a physical therapist helping crippled black children. Hillela goes back initially as part of a relief mission to help civil war victims but also makes it part of the other aspect of her living in the present; therefore, she volunteers to her fiancée when she returns the fact that she has become the lover of Reuel, the guerilla leader (whom she will eventually marry), and "I don't think you'd be able to—well, to manage with that" (*SN*, 263).

Teresa L. Ebert, replying to "essentialist" theoreticians who claim women embody a psychic and mystic sexuality that is female in its essence, has objected that the idea of a cultural revolution of the feminine "will not end the suffering of women; it will not stop the global social, economic, sexual oppression and violence against women. It shifts the site of struggle from socio-economic emancipation to the sensuous maximizing of bodily pleasures and the libidinal liberation of the individual."[27] Despite appreciating the importance of that libidinal liberation, Gordimer and her most favored characters never lose sight of the greater importance of that full social liberation on which other freedoms, including those of the imagination and senses, are likely to depend.

So there are many ways of living in the present. Hannah's cottage, where Sonny lives his other life, is virtually a parody of Rosa's Riviera room but made not for comfort and romance; rather, as observed for the first time by his son, it is put together for the intense frankness of daily unromanticized living, political activism, and sex: "Bare floor and a huge picture like spilt paint that dazzles your eyes, a word-processor, hi-fi going with organ music, twisted stubs in ashtrays, fruit, packets of bran and wheatgerm, crumpled strings of women's underthings drying on a radiator—and a bed, on the floor" (*MSS*, 85). That this is not purely an erotic choice, a preference to be "close to the wood of the floor, the earth beneath it," is perceived by the narrator, who recognizes in it a principle more revolutionary, at least democratic if not anarchic: "Under the softness of the mattress only the law of gravity itself" (*MSS*, 71).

This novel offers us another strong woman for whom the personal and political connect differently. In so doing, it avoids seeming prescriptive or doctrinaire, values the multiplicity of principled responses to what experience teaches us. Aila's late discovery of political commitment, driven by family connections and apparently devoid of sexual involvement, almost trivializes her husband's. Yet the author holds her story at a distance: We get little of it, and she never has a turn as narrator. Pure in its intensity, motivation, and conviction, her political activism is not to be experienced but to be admired. It becomes that which her life is about, replacing the husband, home, and children that her life previously had been about. Silent as always in her own counsel and in her understanding, thorough in her involvement as she has once been in her domestic attentiveness to the meals and carefully ironed shirts, to flowers on the table, she yet seems passive even in commitment, tolerant not only of her husband's sexual treason but also of his sexual failures with her. Notwithstanding that she may have been lied to by her co-activists as well or that her willingness to oblige may have been taken advantage of, Aila's acceptance of this calling is complete. In its singleness, devoid of ambiguous erotic compulsion or the tensions of ego, it does not draw us inside, does not demand that we understand it or the one who embodies it. Still, for that very reason, because Aila will not apologize about the grenades and mines even if she did not know they were going to be secreted at her home, she takes on herself the full implications of her devotion, her faithfulness. Unconcerned by any misgivings about using violence against the violent, she seems to be a spiritual relative of Hillela.

Back from her mission to the areas of conflict, before her devastating revelation to her fiancée, Hillela and Brad quarrel over the dismaying moral complexity of what she has seen, the "ugly confusion" she has accepted as an unescapable reality; consequently, she "took sides in the general horror," thereby outraging his decent liberal conviction that righteous ends cannot be achieved through savage means.

> There were women who had been raped by soldiers and schoolchildren abducted for military training.—By which side?—She wasn't always clear.—And some lied. . . . But if they had been raped and mutilated?—
> —Yes, but some were being fed and looked after by other soldiers. They gave them their own rations. We saw that, too.——It's sickening. And

what kind of decent regime can come out of people like that. . . . That
crowd has to be fought with its own tactics—what else is war? You're a
victim, or you fight and make victims. . . . The others can fight back only
if the rural people support them—even if they have to force them sometimes. (*SN*, 262–63)

By her willingness to be who and what she is both sexually and politically, disturbing though that may be to one's convictions about personhood
and violence, Hillela earns—at least is granted—the redemptive moment,
at the unfurling of "the flag of Whaila's country" (*SN*, 341). Hillela is the
only one of Gordimer's protagonists whose revolution has succeeded: Bray
dies, his work at last published for political use by the president whom he
had turned against; Rosa is jailed; Maureen Smales remains in flight toward the helicopter of some unknown power; the pseudonymous Vusi, Joy,
and Charles are in hiding; Eddie is dead, having cost the Witwatersrand
area several hours of electricity; Will still looks ahead to his coming time
for politics, with his father back in detention and his mother an exile. The
author has said of Hillela, "There *are* people who live instinctively. . . .
And they are great survivors." [28] In this case, survival alone is not enough,
but then Hillela has more, for she survives in a good cause. Instincts allow
her to drill through the cerebrations, to see even the atrocities of her own
side and say, "That's what happens" while retaining her commitment to the
cause.

In an essay published in 1982, Gordimer candidly assessed her own political complicity in remaining silent about repression by one's own side,
reporting her silence (along with all but one of the assemblage) when a
speaker at an international cultural conference in Botswana alleges that
Soviet writers work in "peace and security." Gordimer explains, both to
herself and to us, "I am silent because . . . any criticism of the communist
system is understood as a defence of the capitalist system which has
brought forth the pact of capitalism and racism that is apartheid, with its
treason trials to match Stalin's trials, its detentions of dissidents to match
Soviet detentions, its banishment and brutal uprooting of communities and
individual lives to match, if not surpass, the gulag." [29] Judging herself after
the fact, she declares, "I was a coward and no doubt often shall be one
again," trying to speak and act in "a place of shifting ground forecast for
me in the burning slag heaps of coal mines" she daringly played on in
childhood, the "ugly confusion" through which Hillela navigates by apparently flawless instinct. The notion seems central to Gordimer's view of
contemporary life, principally but not only in South Africa. She has also
spoken of "this constant shifting of foothold" and described her own literary intention as the desire "to convey this constant shifting along, on

very uncertain and uneven ground."[30] That wariness as one moves across the dangerous slag heaps of political allegiances and activities arises from genuine uncertainty of what can be done, what must be done, when the gods have failed.

> Because communism since 1917 has turned out not to be just or human either, has failed this promise even more cruelly than capitalism, have we to tell the poor and dispossessed of the world there is nothing else to be done than to turn back from the communist bosses to the capitalist bosses? In South Africa's rich capitalist state stuffed with Western finance, fifty thousand black children a year die from malnutrition and malnutrition-related diseases, while the West piously notes that communist states cannot provide their people with meat and butter.[31]

Even socialism has its failures, Gordimer admits, although she believes it carries a greater potential for redemption than its rivals. Consequently, "I've become socialist in my general outlook . . . despite the fact that these are the years where one has seen the greatest failures of socialist experiments. . . . I don't believe in perfection; I believe in limited goals."[32] If one's most basic belief is in "the brotherhood of man" and the ultimate question is how to end suffering, Gordimer insists we look into the face of woe and admit the smell of suffering. Confronted with these, ideological rigidity seems a shameful luxury. The colors tinting the dyer's hand form no flag.

CHAPTER FOUR

WEBS OF FALSEHOOD

From a jail cell in Birmingham, Alabama, Martin Luther King, Jr., reminded white clergymen who had reproved his nonviolent campaign against segregation, "We are caught in an inescapable network of mutuality, tied in a single garment of destiny."[1] It is exactly the essential oneness of humanity, shared inevitably by peoples coexisting in one locality and history, that is denied by the law and practice of separateness, apartheid. Like other varieties of bigotry driven by an ideology, apartheid solidifies evanescent or superficial differences into a taxonomy for ranking and excluding. It is the legal embodiment of that ideological rigidity that Gordimer's "sensuous experience" resists.

Separation obstructs our ability to meet and consequently our ability to know one another. So the white woman and African man in Nadine Gordimer's early short story "Is There Nowhere Else Where We Can Meet?" do "meet" only in the tussle of a purse snatching. Instituted separateness casts us in stereotyped roles within a predictable drama yet confounds our capability to fathom our own characters, motives, and behavior. Fulfilling even the necessary duty of being honest about oneself is, we find, more than ordinarily difficult wherever knowledge is considered so dangerous that it must be hedged with division, ignorance, or deception. The garment of mutuality becomes a web of falsehood.

The title of Gordimer's first novel, *The Lying Days* (1953), resonates beyond its original context in a Yeats poem, in which it evoked illusion-laden posings of youth. Among the quandaries to be wrestled with in the book is how to accept that one is part of a societal context even when alienated from it. The novel's protagonist, Helen Shaw, identifies a crucial difference between herself and a fellow South African, a young Zionist confident enough of his self-knowledge to be committed to the land of Israel and its relatively egalitarian kibbutz life. Disgusted with her own country, Helen (conscious of a historical irony) complains, "Now I'm homeless and you're not. . . . The accident of your Jewish birth gives you an excuse for belonging somewhere else" (LD, 351). We, perhaps recalling through such words the "accident" of the author's own Jewish birth, may comprehend that they register some perplexity over the mysteries of happenstance, fate, conscious choice, and commitment. In South Africa perhaps more than elsewhere, liberal or activist whites are caught between two problematic assertions: Rosa Burger's "no one can defect" (BD, 332) and Turgenev's "The honorable man will end by not knowing where to live," which Gordimer uses as the epigraph for A Guest of Honour. The self-aware person caught in this dilemma cannot avoid wondering, who am I and what am I about?

Although Nadine Gordimer's assimilated Jewish parents raised her devoid of contact with Jewish practice or community, she knew that her father and maternal grandparents were immigrants to South Africa who once belonged somewhere else; she may have been aware that traditionally for Jews, living somewhere else has implied as well being in exile from one's ancestral home, ironically the somewhere else to which Helen's Zionist friend is emigrating. Gordimer surely was conscious that other South Africans, not solely Jews, were choosing to leave. She also understood—or at least would acknowledge later—that the economic hopes that drew her mother's parents from England to South Africa and the socioeconomic desperation that led to her father's being sent there at the age of thirteen thrust them willy-nilly into a societal structure they neither made nor intentionally selected.[2] Furthermore, her own artistic and cultural community might well have drawn her also someplace other than her native land. She has long recognized the availability of such an "excuse": In a 1989 interview, she acknowledged that repression in the 1960s led her to consider emigrating to Zambia until her visits showed "that there I was just regarded as a European" rather than "a white African."[3] Politically alienated from her country, she never chose emigration personally or for Helen Shaw. Both women are to be white Africans.

Still, Helen confesses to herself that even the tongues of her native land are foreign to her. "I had grown up, all my life, among strangers; the Africans, whose language in my ears had been like the barking of dogs and the cries of birds" (LD, 186). The protagonists of later books, Rosa Burger and Maureen and Bam Smales (in July's People), must also acknowledge that they never learned the language of those people whom they—whites born, raised, and educated, like their parents and grandparents, in the

southern cusp of Africa—still call "the Africans." Ironically, the ones who
do learn it are, Maureen bitterly remarks, "never people like us, they're
always the ones who have no doubt that whites are superior" (*JP*, 44). For
them, an African language means a job with authority over blacks, not
creating a linguistic community of understanding with them. In a deeply
autobiographical story called "My Father Leaves Home," a European Jewish
immigrant to South Africa quickly "picked up the terse jargon of English
and their languages the miners were taught so that work orders could be
understood. *Fanagalo*: 'Do this, do it like this.' A vocabulary of command.
So straight-away he knew that if he was poor and alien at least he was
white, he spoke his broken phrases from the rank of the commanders to
the commanded: the first indication of who he was, now" (*J*, 62). It seems
that (to evoke Adrienne Rich) "a common language" must be exclusively a
dream unless one has in mind this blunt instrument.

So we grasp why Rosa Burger's self-discovery and self-revelation compel
her to bring to the fore her full given name. Doing so obliges her to acknowledge the paradoxical split within her own heritage, itself the cobbling
together as always of accident and choice. "Rosa" is actually Rosemarie,
named in part for her Afrikaner grandmother. "You thought I must be
named for Rosa Luxemburg. . . . But my double given name contained
also the claim of MARIE BURGER and her descendants to that order of
life, secure in the sanctions of family, church, law—and all these contained
in the ultimate sanction of colour, that was maintained without question
on the domain, dorp and farm where she lay. *Peace. Land. Bread.* These
they had for themselves" (*BD*, 72–73). Possession and privilege gained by
right of birth and color, dispossession and lack of rights endured because of
birth and color: Coming to terms with these polarities implicates Rosa in
the struggle for her own independence and freedom for black South Africans. As the daughter of convicted Communist trade unionists, her father
having died a martyr's death in prison, Rosa is expected to be a revolutionary. Instead, she struggles for an independent life, fighting the presumed
inevitability of revolutionary commitment, and declaring her own independent right to be a private person, at least an individual. The commitment to work for peace, land, and bread for "the Africans" is something
she cannot merely inherit. She must discover her own need for it and work
for it out of a full sense of who and what she is, as Rosa and as Burger's
daughter.

Burger's daughter: her father Lionel's daughter, one supposes, though
she is at the same time the daughter also of Cathy, her mother, a political
activist as well but one who died the private death of multiple sclerosis
outside of prison, not the hero's death inside it. Still, Gordimer—who has
said often that she did not become a political novelist out of preference or

temperament but because one cannot do otherwise in such a country—
shows how the place defines its people, for better or worse. Held suspect
by the South African security apparatus because of her parents, Rosa is a
hero novitiate to antiapartheid activists who presume her to be as devoted
to the struggle as her parents were.

Burger's *daughter:* a daughter rather than a son. Literary and cultural
presumptions would likely oblige a son to be a Telemachus or an Ascanius,
following the footsteps of a heroic father. The daughter might prove an
Antigone but would be excused the choice of an uncommitted life, even if
that meant to "live the life of a white lady." Given Rosa's solid Afrikaner
family tradition, "I don't suppose it's too late for that" (*BD*, 330). In like
manner, Mehring's liberal activist lover has admitted to him that the ran-
dom sight of "a puppy outside one of those little houses with a polished
stoep and ferns in a tin" has given her a moment of longing for that sort
of life; in Mehring's insight, it has been one of those "moments when you
want to submit to the 'system,' keep out of trouble, be a housewife com-
placent in her white privilege" (*CN*, 99). Rosa attempts a different sort of
getaway from political pressures, leaving South Africa for the French Riviera, where she can enjoy something like a bucolic idyll in the midst of
this epic adventure. Falling in love with a politically sympathetic and comfortably married intellectual French journalist, she is tempted by his prop-
osition that she live in Paris as his mistress. Doing so would defy bourgeois
convention but would also spurn revolutionary engagement. It would make
her a woman on the fringe of societal structure, marking a place in opposition to marital custom yet acceding to its societal prerogatives. Rosa's
near-commitment to that plan signifies that she could contentedly choose
a private life outside of South Africa over a life within South Africa that
can never be private, no matter how she might attempt to constitute it.
Her options are different from those of her late brother, one of the ghost
memories populating the book, the probable heir apparent who drowned as
a youth, a victim of his own insecure bravado and the need (his own and
his father's) to be, in more than biological terms, Burger's son.

The moment of personal commitment arrives after a serendipitous
meeting with someone else from her childhood, a surrogate brother, the
child of one of Lionel Burger's black colleagues hiding outside the country,
whom the elder Burger took in and helped to raise. Now a grown man and
only dimly recognizable to her, he is furiously resentful that, even dead,
her white father is the remembered hero, while countless dead black heroes
(his own father among them) are forgotten; he is also angry that her family's ties to individual black people and the black cause make her think that
she can "be different from all the other whites who've been shitting on us
since they came." His ultimate rebuke to her is couched in terms of identity

and names; he has reclaimed his given African name and refuses to acknowledge the nickname by which she knows him, *Baasie*, Afrikaans for "little boss." "I don't know who you are. You hear me, Rosa? You didn't even know my name" (*BD*, 322).

It is significant that this conversation occurs over the telephone during the middle of the night. In *The Conservationist*, Mehring's continual reliance on the telephone and disregard of answering-machine messages disclose how distantly he is connected to his farm, business, and acquaintances. Zwelinzema's call has roused Rosa literally and metaphorically from sleep, as a voice speaking out of the darkness. At this moment she truly cannot see his face, he is separate from her, a presence to be talked at on the other end of an impersonal object through which one cannot meet, cannot see or touch the other person. Still, he is right. She did not know his name nor that it means "suffering land." In fact, she cannot even pronounce it correctly, because—like Helen Shaw and Maureen and Bam Smales—she never learned the language. The medium of the telephone, in which people talk into the receiver, connected only by a thin transmitting line, perfectly expresses the extent to which they can communicate with one another. Nonetheless, the call has come out of her past, out of this present dark void, and out of South Africa but speaking of it, in the accusatory voice of one who has outgrown being patronizingly placated as "little boss" because he is no longer a child and knows that he is no boss.

Because she is reminded again and again that "no one can defect," Rosa returns to South Africa to work in a black hospital as a rehabilitation therapist, making her own kind of contribution to the welfare of black people: "I am teaching them to walk again. . . . They put one foot in front of the other" (*BD*, 332). Though as apolitical in her overt activities as she is political in her convictions, Rosa is jailed in one of the "antiterrorism" sweeps. To the BOSS (Bureau of State Security) she is "Burger's daughter." We recognize that this daughter's independent identity need not be separate from the public one. She has found her individuality through her union with others and her political commitment therapeutically, helping maimed Africans "put one foot in front of the other." Such self-discovery brings both peace and vitality.

She also (paradoxically) gains the privacy and seclusion she had once sought in Europe. This has come unbidden, enforced; still, it may recall Thoreau's dictum about the proper place for the just person in an unjust society. Our last words from her are a cheery postcard message about her jail accommodations, linking her experience not only with that of her parents but also with her idyllic recollections of the Riviera. Our last words about her come from an old family friend who returns from a prison visit remarking that Rosa "looked like a little girl . . . About fourteen"—the age at which we first glimpsed her waiting outside prison with a parcel and a hidden message for her mother, linked to adult womanhood that day both by responsibility and by menarche—"except that she's somehow livelier than she used to be" (*BD*, 360). The word *livelier* is significant. Rosa had said earlier, thinking of her dead father, "I know it's possible to be happy while (I suppose that was so) damaging someone by it. From that it follows naturally it's possible to feel very much alive when terrible things—dread and pain and threatening courage—are also in the air" (*BD*, 351). With something like envy of him, she declares that "you had the elation" (*BD*, 349). Words and phrases such as "feel very much alive . . . in the air . . . elation" suggest how fully Gordimer recognizes the emotional, even erotic, power within the political. She herself has remarked, apropos of *A Sport of Nature*, that sexual and political vigor go together.[4] Rosa, no hedonist, will generate the sensual energy of living from within the cell that encloses her; rejuvenated and lively, she seems virtually born again to her parents, whose story—whether epic or tragic—she again embodies.

To Maureen Smales, one of July's people, the elation never comes, only the dread and pain and something threatening like the need for courage. She and her husband, Bam, white liberals who attempted to participate in interracial dialogue and gave up discouraged (though they always treated the black domestic worker "like one of the family") are rescued by their erstwhile servant, July, when civil war hits Johannesburg at some time in the indefinite future. They find themselves living like black Africans with July's other people, his real family, in the cluster of huts comprising his village. There the children adapt, as always. Bam, an architect by profession, copes in his own way at first; for his family, he can play father on an extended camping trip, and for the villagers, he can be the great white provider, privileged with the technical knowledge to direct construction of a water tank and with possession of a rifle and the skill to use it. Because of what he can offer, Bam is introduced by July into the male social rituals of this different but nonetheless patriarchal culture. If not exactly at home, Bam adapts to the routines and rigors of village subsistence. The familial routines of household life give way to those of camping out. Out here Bam's and July's masculine capability supercedes Maureen's domestic supervision.

Unlike Bam, Maureen has no guide into the spoken or cultural language comprising the village social system. The author's distance from cultural feminist idealism about the common bonds of all women becomes clear from the asymmetry of the couple's village experiences. While Bam's utilitarian presence gives him entry for a time into the male society, Maureen finds among the overworked and segregated women no female society, no community welcoming her as a sister under the skin. She has nothing to offer the African village women, who find her ludicrously ill adapted to the physical demands of those agricultural and domestic tasks that make up their life's work. Within her family and in the village, devoid of any necessary function distinct from those of the African women, she cannot even join them. Their consciousness of color and class transcend affinities of gender.

Further isolating her is the fact that her host, now both protector and supervisor, disapproves of her attempts to socialize with the women. Maureen, angry because July prohibits her from working with his wife, challenges him with the knife edge of what she knows about his previous life, the unmentioned woman who was his lover in town: "Are you afraid I'm going to tell her something?" His furious reply not only confronts but insults her by flinging back the one factual relationship between him and his erstwhile employer. Doing so, July asserts the limits of those facts that they, by social consent, are permitted to know of one another, denying her right to any degree of personal knowledge of him: "What you can tell?—His anger struck him in the eyes.—That I'm work for you fifteen years. That you satisfy with me—" (JP, 98). These are statements, not questions; they do not invite response but close the issue. The pseudo-intimacy fostered through household contact in the white world has become a dangerous liability for them both, and it is their shared knowledge that divides them. If knowledge is power, such power derives only from the ability to use that knowledge as currency. Here Maureen is bankrupt, because her marketable knowledge is both outside what ought to have been her ken and irrelevant to the labor arrangement that July insists on as the essence of their relationship. Reacting against her allusion to his sexual secret, July recalls his ability to "satisfy" her need for his labor; he thereby reestablishes the professional terms of their relationship.[5]

White women likely will know aspects of servants' lives that white men do not see; that is a consequence of the division of roles in such a culture. It is Maureen's place to deal with the servants. She, therefore, is the one to whom they turn for assistance, the one who may become aware of the personal dimensions of their lives, the conditions in which they live, the effects of the disruptions caused in their lives by the agencies of racism. The seer, of course, is also seen, known by both the servants and the observant novelist who shifts her perspective to get a different view, for example, to let us know July's Maureen not only as she sees herself in relation to her former servant, but also to let us see how July sees her and has seen her. Maureen's condescension and mistrust show clearly. For her part, the writer records these along with the differences between white privilege and black necessity.

Maureen has no place. What this means in practice is that she has no occupation, no role or function either inside her family or out. As the one accustomed to July's patois, she has served as a kind of interpreter between him and her husband, but that role has become superfluous and, finally, impossible. She cannot work here, nor can she teach her children what they need to know about living in this environment. She cannot raise her daughter to be a village woman or her son (Victor, whose name now seems more ironic than eponymous) to be a man in this African culture. Such socialization is indeed under way, but it occurs under the guidance of others.[6]

Even more than her husband, who was secure in his flourishing career as an architect with international contacts, Maureen previously looked to a network of societal relationships that gave her a place and a power as mother, community citizen, guardian of the household, and employer, at least of July. In their previous life, "back there," hers was "the name, the authority that signed his pass every month," and she was the one at home—her home—where he worked (*JP*, 145). When their rifle disappears and Bam (whose name no longer suggests jaunty masculinity but rather a bursting balloon) collapses desolate and defeated, it is Maureen who seeks out July, demanding he find the thief and return their property. Here, where possession of a vehicle and gun is everything worth fighting for and the rules are no longer the accustomed ones, the relationship that Maureen had valued between herself and July, a relationship she had mistaken for the intimacy of would-be equals, breaks down, as July reduces and redefines it. "Same like always. You make too much trouble for me. Here in my home too. Daniel, the chief, my-mother-my-wife with the house. Trouble, trouble from you. I don't want it any more. You see?" (*JP*, 151) So Maureen's apparent base of power and authority proves a liability. Precisely because she has been the one to interact with July throughout their time together, she is the one whom he resents. Taking on herself the vain burden of demanding that July recover Bam's gun, she will also suffer July's indignation for doing so. Like the European Jewish petty official subject to the rage of the exploited, the white woman who has been principally an agent will bear the blame for the system of which she has been both beneficiary and pawn.

Earlier, Gordimer showed Rosa Burger striving for identity, beginning with the externally imposed identity that is part of her heritage, her familial legacy, her patrimony. That search seems to bring her full circle, back to a public and political role; however, it is achieved in her own way, not her father's, and on her own terms. The only sense in which it might be heroic is the one to which Adrienne Rich alludes in allying herself

> . . . with those
> who age after age, perversely,
>
> with no extraordinary power,
> reconstitute the world.[7]

Rosa has thought but not about herself, "yes, it's strange to live in a country where there are still heroes" (*BD*, 332). Alas, it is a country that jails its heroes; such is often the way. But it is still possible to be one; the idea and fact have not yet died in that model of South African society.

In *July's People*, though there may be heroes in Maureen Smales's South Africa, we do not see them, and she is not one. (Appropriately, Victor accepts a gift from July with, Stephen Clingman notes, "the prototypical gesture of black obeisance."[8]) A well-intentioned person, she becomes a victim and at the end a woman fleeing. Responding to the sound of a helicopter that has landed nearby, with unknown occupants from an unidentifiable power, "she runs toward it. She runs" (*JP*, 160). So the novel ends, with Maureen in flight toward, but also from—from the dirt and stench, from the primitive, from her own marginality as a social being. What she runs toward is the mechanical emissary of a technological society pulsating with apparently inexhaustible and even primal, terrible energy—nothing more certain than that, nothing more noble than that. "A high ringing is produced in her ears, her body in its rib-cage is thudded with deafening vibration, invaded by a force pumping, jigging in its monstrous orgasm— the helicopter has sprung through the hot brilliant cloud just above them all, its landing gear like spread legs, battling the air with whirling scythes." The helicopter's descent is like a battery and rape, her body "thudded" and "invaded" by the power of something brutal and anonymous: "She could not have said what colour it was, what markings it had, whether it holds saviours or murderers" (*JP*, 158). How desperate she takes her circumstances to be may be judged by that last antithesis, as if anyone not a murderer must be a savior. But that machine pulsates with a presence and meaning that overwhelm the impotent Bam along with the detritus of Maureen's current life, half-sewn shorts, the wattle fowl cage, elephant grass, and thorn thicket, even the bakkie that will run out of fuel and be left to rust. The convictions of this liberal integrationist and would-be power-sharer have dissolved along with her function and purpose as a social being and a human being. She runs at the last "like a solitary animal at the season when animals neither seek a mate nor take care of young, existing only for their lone survival, the enemy of all that would make claims of responsibility." If life means to live on the level of black tribal subsistence,

amid the struggles for power and authority that occur within its relationships, she has no place in it. Simply maintaining oneself becomes exhaust-
ing, unbearable.

Suppose this is what faces white liberalism in the midst of an ongoing
South African revolution, not one in some prophetic time ahead but one
unfolding in the novel's and our own time. Suppose one sees not only a
life devoid of apartheid per se but also one devoid of influence. Suppose
one no longer sees one's own importance and usefulness but faces instead
a life without clear social functions, in the absence of those based on the
old racial divisions of roles and privileges. Suppose one recognizes, through
the prospect of their loss, how much of one's inner sense of selfhood has
been shaped in fact by the impressions of importance, difference, specialness, and refinement attendant upon gifts of arbitrarily defined race and
class "superiority." Suppose the loss of privilege also portends a life without amenities. Suppose that the leaders one is likely to get are the leaders
one has prepared. Suppose that what remain constant are sexual oppression, poverty, and contests for smaller and larger manifestations of power
and control. Therefore suppose, in short, that the future looks like the
present, with the cards merely reshuffled.[9]

"Something Out There," Gordimer's complex novella published in book
form in 1984, three years after July's People, explores the consequences
attending the persistent denial of oneness and failure of progressive reform,
not only in the action and consciousness of the characters but in the form
of the story itself, a representation of a fragmented society breaking apart.
In the course of the previous novels, particularly Burger's Daughter and
July's People, white liberals and radicals had learned what one of her earlier
characters called the discovery of nineteenth-century liberalism, "the par-
adox that playing safe was dangerous" (GH, 391). This lesson they learn
through their schooling in both their own lives and the life of Africa. Commitment, survival, and self-identity all challenge those well-meaning
people striving toward what will be the inevitable failure of a strategy of
playing safe. Because the single garment of destiny has been rent deliberately, the novella's whites live amid "a great diversity of morbid symptoms," not the least of which are the narrowing of commitment, fear for
survival, and loss of identity.[10]

The fragmented narrative point of view and structure of "Something
Out There" depict a South Africa lacking a clear center of coherence or
commonality of perception. Widespread paranoia, distrust, and deception
take their places. Glimpsed in separate vignettes, terrified people respond
in fear and violence to the occasionally sighted menace of a mysterious
humanoid creature on the loose, a dark and furry beast whose forays pro-

vide the news and common concern tying these people together. As if each were compartmentalized by private fear, hostility, secrecy, mistrust, and sense of danger, they neither touch nor communicate with one another.

Even the opposition exists in isolated cells with only local impact. Gordimer's previous explorations of life's main issues in South Africa had centered on individuals, who may not always have been remarkable by themselves but whose literary roles seemed to affirm the significance of the life of the individual. At the heart of this story, by contrast, is an interracial group, two black saboteurs and the two white supporters who provide a cover for their activities. None is a central figure or narrative focal point; no one story is preeminent or even fully known or knowable. The four activists have only an imperfect understanding of one another and of themselves as individuals. In this society what is most important is that which may not or cannot be known, so there is nothing left but violence on one side or the other.

Liberalism has vanished. Long distrustful of the efficacy of liberal reasonableness under unreasonable circumstances, Gordimer seems to erase it completely from the scene in this work. Eschewing the literary device of the single protagonist, she has shifted the center of focus to group action. Although this proved not to be a permanent change in her aesthetic, in this instance it suggests setting aside individualism—the core of liberal politics—as the standard measurement of social importance or achievement. Each member of the sabotage cell has a story and a personality, yet the author concentrates on their functional relations with one another, not their intrinsic individual interest. If the absence of a main protagonist implies that there is no discernible central consciousness and focus of our concern, perhaps (at least under certain circumstances) highlighting such a center is misleading or fraudulent. All the stories need to be heard on their own terms. Celebrating a Bray, a Burger, or even a Zwelinzima, is neither the issue nor the answer. Frequently the stories from the late 1980s and early 1990s published in *Jump* use multiple narrators or narrative viewpoints to express fundamental dichotomies in experience and perception, acknowledging that one point of view affords a limited, false understanding; consequently, a story about a political prisoner's release needs to be two narratives, his wife's and his own ("Amnesty"), and a mother and her children returning home to Africa are seen from the very different angles of vision afforded by another airline passenger, the thirteen-year-old son who has taken on adult responsibilities, and the husband-father awaiting them at the airport, conscious of his treacheries, guilt, eagerness, and marginality ("A Journey").

Also gone is verbally articulated political radicalism, now driven underground—literally, into the abandoned mine where Eddie and Vusi prepare for their raid on the electrical power station. Arguments, debates, interior monologues, quoted speeches, and pamphlets rehearsing current South African progressive and radical viewpoints appeared frequently in the author's fiction heretofore, sometimes (as with *Burger's Daughter*) in clear defiance of the country's stringent political censorship. There is no place for such forms of public political opposition where there is no place for shared ideas or acceptance for inconvenient knowledge. With macabre appropriateness, eighteen months after "Something Out There" was published, the South African government's State-of-Emergency legislation expanded to nearly unparalleled repressiveness, clamping an iron mask of silence on both political discussion and the exchange of political information.

It is with the issue of knowledge, and particularly self-knowledge, that the dispassionate, clear-voiced narrator concludes. We find not just that "nobody really knows" who the subsequently killed Eddie actually was. More importantly, "nobody really knows . . . whom they believe themselves to be, the three who survived and disappeared. Nobody really knows which names mark the identity each has accepted within himself. And even this is not known fully to himself, all that brought him to this pass; this place, this time, this identity he feels" (*SOT*, 202). Not mere ignorance but a radical ignorance of roots and essential identity unfolds as the narrator searches out undiscovered genealogies and histories in the patchwork past of South Africa's land and people that the story itself touches on. People do not know their ancestry, "too confused by the linguistic and cultural exchanges of treks and intermarriage to keep records." Worse, they do not even know the true history of the place in which they live and about which they fight. "No one knows," the narrator cagily concludes, that "centuries before time was measured," this abandoned mine was the site of another, where "metals precious to men were discovered, dug and smelted, for themselves, by black men" (*SOT*, 203).

That phrase, "no one knows," resonates significantly in Gordimer's work. "No one knows where the end of suffering will begin," she wrote in *Burger's Daughter* (356). In that earlier work, however, the phrase reflected on the limitations of all human knowledge, the shortsightedness that comes along with being mortal. In the later one, part of the final cadential survey of what "no one knows," it testifies to the broken, despoiled, buried history of a land in which one begins by not knowing the truths about one's country and ends by not knowing oneself. In "The Moment Before the Gun Went Off," a more recent, painfully ironic story with an O. Henry twist, an Afrikaner farmer internationally excoriated for the accidental shooting death of a young African farm laborer cannot defend himself or seek public sympathy because he must keep silent about his past offense. "How could they know that *they do not know*. Anything. The young black callously shot through the negligence of the white man was not the farmer's boy; he was his son" (*J*, 117). The South African situation is a particularly intensified paradigm of human experience. Throughout her career, Gordimer has seen South Africa, but not South Africans, as a special case; their deceptions, commitments, and losses remind us of how much all of us have in common. When the daughter in "My Father Leaves Home" returns to that home, we discover only at the end that it is not in fact his village, the name of which she has never known: "He never told me; or I didn't listen." Furthermore, in the graveyard, "the script that records their names is a language he forgot and his daughters never knew" (*J*, 66, 65). Even the lineage that connects us to other places, other times, and other families in a great web of mutuality is severed. The accusing voices protest, "You didn't even know my name. . . . No one knows."

Even when we know the truth, we may fail, deliberately or unthinkingly, to communicate it. The author once wrote of the phenomenon using an image perhaps deriving from her mining-town background but certainly attesting to her continuing concerns about what is hidden, what we do not disclose or admit. "It's part of living in South Africa, having these incredible layers of concealment. . . . What we say and do—well, it's always only half of what we mean, but in South Africa it's less than half." [11] A more direct form of activism may seem all that is left, as it does to Joy and Charles, the white colleagues of the saboteurs Vusi and Eddie in "Something Out There." Helpful and dedicated as go-between and gofer, they remain awkward and unskillful in their dealings with their black comrades, whose language and lives remain separate and distinct from them; the four are united only in their willingness to risk prison or death. They will hit a target that is vulnerable, isolated across the veld, and convenient. They may serve another unstated and more profound goal, though, in attacking such a target, a goal we can comprehend by thinking of Maureen heading toward a helicopter that attests only to a technically advanced culture somewhere out there. To strike at that kind of power and make it nonfunctional, to interrupt the comforts of the whites' way of life, to cut off the whites' power is to carry the revolution where it needs to be felt. In its own right it is as powerfully symbolic an act as Ralph Ellison's invisible man clandestinely draining electricity to fill his basement with sound and light, thereby giving presence to his life. The saboteurs mean to fill white space with blackness, with an absence that attests in its small way to the vacancies that make up black subsistence in South Africa. This is the most poetic undermining of state security, the most immediate challenge to power. If the "network of mutuality" is denied, why not attack the power grid?

What they achieve is not exactly a major victory, although it is a success. Power is out for eighteen hours; no one knows anyone else any better;

Eddie will eventually be killed; little has been communicated through action other than the urgency of the situation and the insecurity of white power. One works, necessarily, with such "terrible tools" as circumstance allows (*SOT*, 203).

Within the inner relationships of this interracial (and yet still racially divided) group, Gordimer shows the subtle difficulties posed by divided histories. Notably, it is the one woman in the group who helps bridge the gap at some basic level, deeper than Charles does, despite his sharing manual labor alongside his black colleagues. "She was the one who came out bluntly with things that detached the four of them from their separate, unknown existences behind them and the separate existences that would be taken up ahead, and made a life of their own together, in this house and yard" (*SOT*, 144). Such a role seems remarkable because Joy is a marginal character in this story, yet the author suggests that she, by language, both deconstructs and reconstructs their reality. Joy's plain-speaking candor breaks down the divisions between them, temporarily uniting them in a way that political sympathies and commonality of risk do not. It is perhaps this function that justifies thinking of her name as anything more than ironic or, at best, caprice.

The exchange precipitating the comment about Joy deals with food.[12] Grocery shopping is her domestic responsibility: The conspirators remain in this way captives of the conventionality amidst which they themselves must pass for conventional. Nevertheless, she resists cooking for all the men as an African woman would do. Her shopping is at least as much attributable to preserving an appearance of normalcy essential to the group's covert activities as it is an unmasking of the continuance of sexual divisions of labor within the resistance movement. Joy's refusal to serve as cook strikes the black Africans as peculiar and annoying but is accepted. They do object, however, to her food selections; it is the older, more experienced of the two who, in the midst of this struggle for other rights, insists as well on the right to his own kind of meat. In their safe house, he takes the authority to protest directly to the white woman. Their major demands are for "real" meat (Joy, a vegetarian, has loosened her principles enough to buy them sausages) and for mealie-pap instead of rice. "Oh, Charles and I like mealie-pap too. But I thought you'd be insulted, you'd think I bought it specially for you" (*SOT*, 144). Neither eloquent nor subtle, she is candid enough to admit (as few openly will) the contortions of imbedded racist thinking. She has been so concerned to avoid seeming racially condescending toward people she will help but does not yet feel comfortable with that she condescends. On a smaller scale, she has replicated the self-sacrificing self-effacement of racial condescension shown by Boaz in *Occasion for Loving* when he accepts his wife's black lover precisely because he is black, leading Jessie to remark, "He's so afraid of taking advantage of Gideon's skin that he ends up taking advantage of it anyway by refusing to treat him like any other man" (*OL*, 288).

Exposing Joy's faux pas, Gordimer affirms the material connection between experience and understanding. In *A Sport of Nature*, it is Hillela's physical sense of life that allows her to understand and transcend the historical importance of "skin and hair," to feel that the body's responses are the surest truths. Hillela's sexual openness and especially sexual responsiveness to the black leaders with whom she becomes involved has been seen by some readers as playing to the old mythology of black/white sexual relations. There is more at work here, however. We recall, for instance, how Gordimer's alertness to sexuality's significance allows her to comment incisively on fear of blacks in Millin's writings. Connecting the physical and political leads Rosa Burger to take up the revolutionary cause as a physiotherapist working with black people, assisting the disabled to walk. If that can be seen as part of a metaphoric exploration of political activism—enablement, literally helping the black independence movement by helping people to put one foot in front of the other—it is as if political theory is the metaphor, this the reality.

Joy wrongly suppressed her home sense. That food should precipitate the honest exchange is not whimsical. Food, after all, is unfalsifiably real, perhaps in some circumstances constituting the only exchange or offering that is. So, in "Comrades," the white political sympathizer who takes home and feeds a group of young black activists realizes the futility of her attempts at amiable social conversation and showing an interest in them: "Only the food that fed their hunger was real" (*J*, 96). What people eat or don't eat and how says much about their cultural identity, whom they think or know they are. Home cooking is the one element of culture that can most easily be sustained after the suppression of one's literature, traditions, and religion (as the Inquisition knew when it hauled in for torture and execution converts from Judaism who were accused of not eating pork). Like one's own language, it is also particularly missed by exiles. In "My Father Leaves Home" the narrator speculates, "Perhaps they had offered to send a girl out for him, a home girl with whom he could make love in his own language, who would cook according to the dietary rules" (*J*, 62). That the father has already married a different sort of "home girl"—"a young woman whose mother tongue was English"—reveals how far he has journeyed, how thoroughly he has adapted to another home.

As Gordimer's recollection about her parents' caution that she was not to drink from the black servant's cup attests, abstract thought or ideology may provide a context for understanding but is not a substitute for experiential knowledge of one another. Such knowledge must lead beyond both the physical revulsion implied by Gordimer's parents and the timidity of Joy's rice.

Joy's ego does not get in her way, however. She has the honesty and grace to recognize and admit what has happened. As she breaks the boundary of unspoken thought, communication begins; out of that emerges briefly a cohesive family of sorts, bizarre and imperfect as any yet united in purpose. Here is a model of interracial cohesiveness for a common purpose. The whites are not in charge; they assist the blacks, who are undertaking the most active, daring role and who will use the munitions that stand for power. On a small scale Joy's act of candor performs the work Kafka described in a statement that Gordimer cites elsewhere: "A book should be an icepick to break up the frozen seas within us." [13]

Those frozen seas are part of apartheid's legacy. We cannot posit that Joy is an authorial surrogate here, deliberately breaking the ice and so letting people flow together into one social whole. She never has any pretensions to the sort of perceptual grasp that the author herself reveals. Still, Joy plays an essential cultural role in the pseudofamily of this work, a role Gordimer connects with women. Minor character though she is, Joy significantly demonstrates that one can transcend one's limiting circumstances through frankness.

Notwithstanding the author's inclinations not to identify herself as a feminist and to see feminism as a subsidiary issue in South Africa, Gordimer's honest observations of experience lead her to recognize that particular circumstances stimulate, shape, direct, or confine women's lives differently from men's, affording them at times special capacities or opportunities within the network of human communications. In another interview, having quoted François Mitterrand as saying that building socialism is a cultural challenge, she continued, "I think black women are close to the young in the black consciousness movement in that they see the emancipation of blacks, black freedom, not only as a political and one might almost say military problem, but also as a cultural one. In their homes, in their . . . values, that's what I mean, in human values . . . they are extraordinarily strong—I often find myself in awe of this tremendous spirit of black women." [14] Seeing women's strength as home-centered and residing in moral and cultural values is an old and essentially traditional concept of female power; we might be reading a testimonial from a half-century ago, even in the almost romanticized celebration of black women's "spirit." Yet on the other hand one might also want to identify in this a racially aware testimony to a *culture féminine,* or *culture féminine noire.* If not essentialist, it may still be pragmatic. In that same interview, Gordimer also comments with a more clearly feminist awareness on the real lives and possibilities of black women in the resistance movement.

> The emancipation of [black] women from their second-rate state—firstly as black and secondly as women—was beginning to come about naturally

within the movements. Women were big and important in the old ANC, a real force. People like Lilian Ngoyi were really very special; but when the movements were crushed and when they emerged underground in a different form somehow there was less place for women; they became supportive again. . . . If you look back . . . fifteen years you realize how much ground black women have lost in South Africa since the mass movements were banned.[15]

Strength emerges, the author implies, where and how it can. She has also noted that in the frontier mentality of South Africa as she was growing up, "culture was a thing for women, and so was liberalism; so was social concern."[16] If the struggle is not only political and military but also cultural, then the third is the one in which women have been the warriors. Suppressed into apparent marginality by political, economic, and social structures, women center their activities where they must, and that becomes a center. As the parenthetic remark "firstly as black and secondly as women" implies, for Gordimer the struggle always is necessarily a racial struggle foremost.

July's People suggests that the honest commerce of mutual knowledge may not be possible within the ordinary constrictions of apartheid society. Still, within that society women may come closer than white men through the domestic relations and knowledge existing between mistress and servant, who at least experience together the multiple dimensions, the doubleness and more of our social behavior, self-perceptions, and self-deceptions. Experience is not understanding, but it has its own limited propaedeutic potential. The female artist and dissident, keyed to the concealments, can reveal the layers. Again, speaking of her narrative technique, Gordimer says, in language characteristically physical and geological (indeed, using a metaphor explicitly from mining),

> if you are drilling straight ahead, so to speak, you are constantly slipping and glancing off what is in the person, off the true center of their motivation and the conglomeration of circumstances and inherited attitudes that make up the inner personality. . . . In order to grasp a subject, you need to use all the means at your disposal: the inner narrative, the outer, the reflection on an individual from other people, even the different possibilities of language, the syntax itself, which takes hold of different parts of reality.[17]

The icepick attack on the frigid seas won't help with polysemous reality. To work so probingly and spaciously in and around a character and culture demands a freedom or the illusion of it, hard to come by in an apartheid culture. It is less a freedom of expression than a freedom to perceive, an opportunity to hear, to know, to see, to grasp what the experience of life seems like to people who know a different range of it than oneself and people of one's own background or milieu. That freedom is approximated by the attentive artist, and (differently) by people who must acquire something of an artistic sensitivity to the nuances of language, gesture, and appearance or by those for whom familiarity breeds a kind of intimacy.

In "Blinder," one of the stories in *Something Out There*, Gordimer explores the issues of power and responsibility as they emerge among three women: the white mistress, the black servant who has been the "town woman" of another employee recently killed in an accident, and the rural wife of the dead man. In the story's concluding scene, the widow unexpectedly appears, having taken a monstrous journey with her children from the "location" to the city to claim the man's company pension, which she may never get. (This itself is a more personal version of the government-manipulated theft of the man's ancestral property through the Bantustan scheme.) The widow becomes a figure of tragic dignity, not mute in reality but mute to us because we can in no way grasp her language or know all that she could speak about her experience.

Within the white household, Rose, the servant who is used to being ingratiating and seeming in control of all that takes place within her domain, assumes the duty of protector for her late lover's family. She is accustomed to making sacrifices in her life but acts here out of compassion and loyalty to a woman and children in dire need, people who actually have less than her little. Her heroism involves both financial and emotional sacrifices; it also expresses itself through social and pragmatic control of both of the other women. The lady of the house, aloof but not unfeeling, is left to deal with the social awkwardness without making anyone feel awkward, trying to seem gracious without giving anything away, while her husband sits vacant-faced with their children and guests at the dinner table, remote from the human drama occurring before him, secure behind the protective shield of his wife, who will deal with it. Her function is to be a barrier between the lives of these black people and the lives of the whites behind her at the table, those who will have nothing to do with the matter. In a series of almost codelike verbal exchanges, Rose mediates the terms of her own financial sacrifice and communicates the gestures of respect that will conserve the other women's dignity within their disparate cultures.

The first story in *Something Out There*, "A City of the Living, a City of the Dead," places us in a totally different social environment but, still concentrating on the domestic repercussions of apartheid, it invites us to know something of it from the angle of vision of one whose life is domestically bound and seems remote from political activism. The work is set in the tight, crowded confines of a tiny apartment in a township house. Into this cramped space, shared by a married black couple and their infant as well as impinged upon by a constant procession of neighbors, comes a man on the run, a saboteur whom the husband shelters for political loyalty. While there, the fugitive becomes part of the family in ways only the wife perceives; of the three main characters, she is the only one whose thoughts we are allowed to overhear to complement the narrator's account.

> We are alone together. The baby likes him. I don't give the breast every time, now; yesterday when I was fetching the coal he fed the bottle to her. I ask him what children he has? He only smiles, shakes his head. . . . He comes into the kitchen, now, and helps me when I'm washing up. He came in this morning, and put his hands in the soapy water, didn't say anything, started cleaning up. Our hands were in the grease and soap, I couldn't see his fingers but sometimes I felt them when they bumped mine. He scraped the pot and dried everything. I didn't say thanks. To say thank you to a man—it's not a man's work, he might feel ashamed.
>
> He stays in the kitchen—we stay in the kitchen most of the day with the baby. (*SOT,* 18–19)

Yet even though we are allowed some experience of her consciousness, we are left with a mystery about her. Without offering an explanation—indeed, admitting that she cannot explain the action herself—the woman walks to the police station and reports the man. If we have presumed that we know what she has been thinking, we may be surprised to discover that we did not know how she thinks.

The text suggests many possible explanations. For one, the continuing presence of this wanted man turns an already appallingly confined space into a veritable prison, at least for the wife and mother, lacking her husband's opportunities to go out. The man is also a threat in other ways, having broken not only the state's laws but also the social laws separating one gender's behavior from the other's—the hand that cleans the gun also feeds the baby and scrubs pots. She does not know how to deal with him. He therefore becomes quadruply threatening to her. He takes away her domestic role, changes the patterns of her private life and marital life, claims part of the kitchen space that had been specially hers, and at last threatens her with the stirrings of intimacy as their hands touch in the opaque grease and soap.

These intrusions on her limited environment do not open it outward but constrict it more, threatening what is already there. Her instinctive response reveals much about sociopolitical behavior. She protects what she has and knows, becoming an agent of the state, in essence working for her oppressor and against her liberation. In the exigencies of her immediately pressing life, she rids herself of that which threatens the only security she has. She guards the doorway.

She cannot perceive—and Gordimer permits us to sense why—her kinship with this man, who in taking on the same domestic tasks as she becomes more than a fitting companion and helpmate, something of an androgynous double to her, joining her at her kitchen table, feeding the baby, and washing the dishes at her side. Their lives should merge, this burdened woman and this outlaw man for whom sex-sterotyped roles (even in a society so heavily weighted with them) have become irrelevant. They share namelessness, the woman and the revolutionary who cannot be named. One lives on the margins of society, the other has chosen to cross the borders of acceptability; they demonstrate the linkage between gender and race, making even more poignant and understandable the one victim turning on the other in response to the struggle to exist inside the pressure cooker of a racist and sexist culture. They communicate inadvertently with a frighteningly disruptive touch, and the ultimate betrayal arises from motives so deeply hidden from the betrayer that she cannot find them. They are divided by that which was created to divide, apartheid, aparthood.

Cooking rice instead of mealie-pap, touching hands unintentionally in murky dishwater, gathering to one's view the tones of "black" skin; such details of personal relationships open the culture to us, peel away the layers of concealment, show us again how the personal is political. Especially in those works that decentralize the narrative vision and deny single, autocratic "truth," Gordimer's writing teaches us how to recognize and internalize the experiences of others, to hear the voices of those who cannot or will not write their own stories, to see through the eyes of those whose angles of vision have never been central to the culture and whose place on the margin, in the borderlands, or in the doorway is equivocal. She acknowledges that for all of us who are, for one reason or more, on the margin, in the borderlands, or at the doorway, the decision to open or close the door, to go in or out, to cross over or not, is not always our free choice to make, but the moment of choice cannot be avoided forever. "No one can defect."

CHAPTER FIVE

NO ONE KNOWS

 Unfolding the consequences of hidden knowledge and of betrayals is a motivating force throughout Nadine Gordimer's works, a principle so persistent and so expressive of moral rigor that the term *motif* seems barely sufficient. It is as prevalent in works set outside of African political contexts as those centered in them and in writings devoted to private relationships as much as those explicitly directed toward sociopolitical perceptions.

We have seen the importance Gordimer places on exposing the betrayals and treachery by which we negotiate our relations with others. We have also seen that coming to terms with our own deceptions is an essential stage leading to an honest commitment, at least to one another. A direct complement to this idea, as this chapter will show, is the perception that hidden or evaded knowledge also prevents our connecting with one another. "It's part of living in South Africa, having these incredible layers of concealment, and I suppose I've become more and more conscious of them in relation to other people, and even to myself. . . . What we say and do— well, it's always only half of what we mean, but in South Africa it's less than half." [1] The artist sees her task in this regard also as uncovering the hidden truths within individuals and their society. Again she reminds us that South Africa is a special case but not in kind, only in degree.

Gordimer's work exposes two forms of concealment. One, delineated in the closing paragraphs of "Something Out There," is the systemic suppression or loss of knowledge, which permits inconvenient realities to be dropped from view and histories inscribed so as to give only the desired shape to transmitted knowledge, burying the truths too politically or emotionally dangerous to be articulated. The other is the avoidance of self-examination, the concealment she exposes (for instance) in Mehring, which he at last cannot escape; this is the concealment that Christa Wolf has termed "the mortal sin of our time: the desire not to come to grips with oneself."②

In *A Sport of Nature* the first sort of concealment turns Hillela into a quasi-mythic historical figure about whom no one, including the reader, can know everything. A half-lit world of hearsay and uncertainty is evoked repeatedly in the novel. Even near the end, "no-one knows for sure whether Hillela has had any children as the President's wife; whether she ever had any children other than the namesake" (*SN*, 310). Easily changing one's identity, as "Kim" becomes "Hillela" who becomes "Chiemeka," may threaten the possibility of coming to grips with oneself, but suppose there is no self to come to grips with other than a self responding to the immediacy of experience and moving in an apparently effortless evolution of selfhood from a pseudo-posh Anglo-bourgeoisie eventually to full Africanization? One of the signs of the president's genius—like Hillela, he possesses "a highly intelligent intuition" (*SN*, 310)—is that he realized from the first "that Hillela is a past mistress of adaptation." She acts so much by instinct that she is able to come to grips with herself by having no privileged secrets or hidden agendas; there is no avoidance of self-examination, because no other self lies buried beneath the one that is always open and accessible. She seems suffused with self-knowledge; for Gordimer, self-knowledge carries self-empowerment with it.

The book shares this theme with the novella "Something Out There," *July's People*, and *My Son's Story*. The more conflicted main characters of these works are not endowed with Hillela's equipoise, however. The novella is a study of the power that deception, ignorance, and uncertainty hold over the mindscape of an entire country. Indeed, the work examines what happens emotionally in the tense space between the power of the secret and the power of the knowledge.

The presence of something dangerous just beyond our reach of certainty begins to assume a shape when a thirteen-year-old named Stanley Dobrow photographs, or so he believes, a mysterious rampaging creature ("dark face with 'far-back' eyes") terrorizing the Johannesburg suburbs. His picture actually shows the "thrashing together of two tree-tops," thus spoiling his attempt to document the reality of this creature and provide a means of identifying what it is. As if acknowledging the uncertainty, an editor kills the word "predator" from the newspaper headline, substituting "wild animal" and a question mark (*SOT*, 118). Both words and pictures are confirmed to be imperfect guides to a reality people attempt to constitute according to their own partial knowledge and fragmentary theories based on remembered snippets of folklore and natural history: To one person, the creature is a civet cat, to another "almost certainly" a vervet monkey, to still others "most likely" something larger in the ape family. All such theories are propounded in the papers.

But who can believe what they read, given that texts are as susceptible as anything else to alteration and misunderstanding? "Stanley's name, which had lost a syllable when his great-grandfather Leib Dobrowsky landed from Lithuania in 1920, was misspelt as 'Dobrov'" (*SOT,* 118–19). In this brief and seemingly gratuitous gesture, Gordimer links this particular enigmatic sighting with the train of misinformation and misdirection that gives the lie to what we know. (An almost too tantalizing irony exists in the fact that Gordimer had always erroneously believed that her own father had come from Lithuania.) To a quartet of physicians who surprise the creature in the woods during their golf game, it is either "'one of the black out-of-works' . . . 'a black having a crap, exactly,'" or a baboon (*SOT,* 126). That the latter opinion, advanced by an orthopedic surgeon, proves correct is not really significant except in documenting that the creature is less harmful and volitional than people fear. It seems never to be what it seems to be; but then, who does?

What is "out there" is all that is or may be dangerous, the fearful menace of the day's news, as sensed by the good Afrikaner housewife in whose home two young white people will sit to talk with her husband about a house rental, pretending to be everything they are not. Not Australian; South African. Not married; ex-lovers, now merely comrades. Not settling in the country while they await the birth of the child, because Anna (actually named Joy) is not pregnant; they are providing cover for the two black saboteurs (ostensibly farmhands) who will destroy the power station whose towers are visible from the rental property. The usual "news, these days," tells of troubles and betrayals at home and abroad, "exchanges of insults between factions of what used to be a power to be relied upon, disputes over boundaries that had been supposed to divide peace and prosperity between all," enough to make Mrs. Klopper long even more for the good old days, "before the papers started calling blacks 'Mr' and publishing the terrible things Communists taught them to say about the white man" (*SOT,* 119). Who can believe what they read or trust appearances?

Paradoxically, everything in this land is both deceptive and overdetermined. During its meanderings and marauding, the creature startles a couple having a tryst in a vacant rural cottage. They have resorted to this place because motels seem too sordid, and nicer hotels hold the danger of discovery (for though they are discreetly unnamed and unidentified by the narrator, the man is prominent enough for them to worry about the effect of a possible scandal on his career). With his wife out of the country, he longs to take his lover to his own bed. "But you are never alone in this country. They are always there; the houseboy, the gardenboy mowing the lawn. They see everything; you can only do, in the end, what is all right for them to see and remember. . . . Even his room, his own bed, in a house where he paid for everything—nothing is your own, once you are married." In a previous time of desperation, parking by an old mine dump, they had employed her car, "which her husband had given her, only a month before, new, to please her, because he had become aware, without knowing why, he couldn't please her anymore. She, too, had nothing that was her own; her husband paid for everything that was hers" (*SOT*, 140–41). So the one who pays for everything and the one who is given everything are alike in that neither has anything that is truly their own; amid their privileges—her new car, his large house "in a lair of trees," the love nest with its clean bed and the refrigerator stocked with ice for their whiskey, her "wisp of nylon and lace" and his "beautiful Italian linen trousers," their extramarital relationship itself—their lives seem boundless, except that neither feels free. The betrayed spouses exist only as threats of discovery: He worries, "what would happen to her if her husband found out and divorced her?" and she frets, "in her sense of responsibility for his career, what would happen if his wife found out and made a scandal" (*SOT*, 140). Each, we should notice, is concerned about the other's future, not about the consequences to himself or herself; yet this is surely ironic, self-protective altruism, a reversal of the model helpmate's selflessness, because their concerns betray the unarticulated and covert recognition that, despite their professions of love, their relationship will not continue indefinitely, and if the affair is discovered, neither intends to come to the other's emotional or practical rescue. She, declaring him to be "her first and last lover," is not disillusioned to get no similar assurance from him, understands that she will face "some day—their last afternoon."

When the noise at the window reveals another presence to them, her terrified response, which he attempts to quell, is, "She's hired someone to follow you." Privacy is despaired of, and yet the experience is mysterious because the clues do not suggest the spying of a private detective. The woman heard a sound, "a laugh. A horrible little coughing laugh," which first humiliates her so that he must comfort her not by denying that they could have been observed but rather "denying . . . that they could ever be something to laugh at" (*SOT*, 142). In other words, he rejects not the fact of observation but the interpretation of it. She next reinterprets the laugh to be a "suppressed exclamation of pain" caused by the thorns of the bougainvillea outside the window; later, when they find the half-eaten green fruit betraying the intruder as a hungry animal, the man too claims to have heard a sound, "Not a laugh. A sort of bark or cough" (*SOT*, 142–43). Just as others "see" something that they interpret by their own lights, so these two hear something capable of multiple interpretations in the absence of certain knowledge and the pressure of their own fears. Their relationship, which "she industriously shored up against illusions of any kind," has been discovered but not found out; it is undermined by the forced confrontation that here—even here—they may be vulnerable to prying but are not yet faced with the endgame. The beast "out there" is simultaneously nothing to fear and everything that they fear.

The link between fear of the creature and fear of black people is only tangential in that episode, Africans being represented merely through the man's domestic servants, whom he sees as oppressive restrictions on his liberty because of what they might "see and remember," their knowledge of his life potentially giving them a power over him or over the whites' way of life. The connection is more strongly suggested in other confrontations—with the physicians, for example, or when Police Sergeant Chapman's bride calls him between his sessions interrogating a political detainee to report the theft of a leg of venison from the pantry window: A fellow officer chides, "Some black took it," and another recommends teaching the wife to use a gun. "Next time it might be more than a monkey out there in the yard. Sergeant Chapman ought to know the situation" (*SOT*, 159–60). Sergeant Chapman knows but when he is away from the interrogation rooms in John Vorster Square, he wrestles with the mystery that compels his attention, having worked in his official capacity on these whites who oppose the government: "What more does a white man want? With a black man, all right, he wants what he can't have, and that can make a man sit eating his heart out in jail half his life. . . . There's something wrong with all these [white] people who become enemies of their own country. . . . They're enemies because they can't enjoy their lives the way a normal white person in South Africa does" (*SOT*, 156). So his answer to the mystery of political activism answers nothing but complacently denigrates white activists as perverse. Out there are the really dangerous ones, as he warns his wife, hearing that she imprudently searched with the dog for the thief: "They'll knife you if you try to catch them. . . . I'm telling you, Mariella, you make me worry. There must be blacks hanging around the neighborhood who know I'm often away late." This time, however, he is persuaded it truly was an animal: "Even a black's not going to tear raw meat with his teeth" (*SOT*, 159).

As we see and hear repeatedly in "Something Out There," apartness means (or seems to mean) lack of knowledge about one another; this, according to the dominant myth of white history, derives from the absence of familiar contact between the races. That purported absence both justifies and contributes to the notion that the races must develop separately. The myth is, of course, fraudulent, as Gordimer has often insisted: In so many ways, black individuals and white individuals touch one another (not only physically but metaphorically, through the economy, for instance) or surreptitiously observe one another. Yet it does have validity in the convenient way in which one can avoid knowing, can pretend to be unknown and not to know, can be deprived of knowing and also deprived of consciousness that one does not know. Thus, the man Rosa Burger knew as Baasie can challenge her with the fact that "You didn't even know my name." At the same time he can reject her with a remark that is less a dismissal of her than a tribute to the divisive power of the system they were raised within and raised against functioning within him: "I don't know who you are" (*BD*, 322). If neither knows who the other is, each can become the resentful figure of the other's imagination. We can hear this taking place in these conversations over the phone line:

> I'm not your Baasie, just don't go on thinking about that little kid who lived with you, don't think of that black "brother," that's all.—(*BD*, 321)

> You want something. If it's money, I'm telling you there isn't any. (*BD*, 322)

> The way you look in my mind is the way my [dead] brother does—never gets any older. . . . Might have been killed in the bush with the Freedom Fighters. Maybe I thought that.—
>   —Yeh, you think that. I don't have to live in your head. (*BD*, 323)

As Rosa subsequently perceives, "In one night we succeeded in manoeuvering ourselves into the position their history books back home have had ready for us—him bitter; me guilty. What other meeting-place could there have been for us?" (*BD*, 330). Her words echo the title of one of the author's best-known early writings, the one which begins her own *Selected Stories*, "Is There Nowhere Else Where We Can Meet?" Directly confronting the fearsome racial mythology of physical violence that pits black men against white women, that story focuses on an incident in which a white woman, attempting to suppress her fear at the approach of a physically ravaged-looking, obviously impoverished black man, is in fact mugged. Having tenaciously but unsuccessfully fought him, she hesitates and then decides not to report the incident; vividly aware of what the physical signs have told her about his life in contrast to hers, she cannot bring herself to collude with the racial stereotyping of black male violence, allowing herself this time to be the victim, indeed, holding herself guilty for having fought him over the money.

In a different fashion, Rosa has been assaulted by a black man; she too sees the marks of oppression on her attacker, so that recognizing her privilege takes the place of naming his guilt. Thinking of her taunt to him about money (in what again seems a covert recall of the earlier work), she does not perceive this as "the response to the criminal hold-up, but as the wail of someone buying off not a threat but herself" (BD, 330). The woman in "Is There Nowhere Else Where We Can Meet," recalling the man's "red eyes, and the smell and those cracks in his feet, fissures, erosion," instinctively resisted that "buy off" during the assault but finally yielded to it when the alternative was to align herself with the oppressive state. She suppresses a truth touching her own experience because of the truth that continually touches every aspect of his life (Sel, 20). Rosa's stronger mettle will energize her into activism and send her back to South Africa to immerse herself in the lives of the black children whose bodies have been damaged by the multiple forms of racist violence. Coming back to Africa, she redefines her relationship with her country by choosing physical involvement, eschewing (even if not consciously) flawed political or ideological conceptualizations in favor of the touch.

Rosa's and Zwelinzema's specific moments of critical challenge to their consciousnesses connect on this level with that of Jessie, the most analytic character in Occasion for Loving. Similar to Rosa's unexpected reunion with her childhood friend at a party, Jessie comes upon Gideon, the abandoned black lover of her married friend Ann. Drunk, Gideon initially (as Zwelinzema has complained of Rosa) does not know who she is, but finally, "his gaze recognized something, though perhaps it was not her." His reaction reduces her to a color and gender, characteristics in which they are all alike: "White bitch—get away." He subsequently forgets the episode. Jessie, however, knows that what has been revealed but not acknowledged has not gone away, it simply lies submerged, waiting; therefore, "So long as Gideon did not remember, Jessie could not forget" (OL, 307–8).

Psychologically valid and fitting as Jessie' position is, we might see it as an appropriate alternative response to the character in the earlier story's acceptance of victimization as well as to Rosa's willingness to transcend the personal by gaining political understanding from the event. In the historical context of Gordimer's fiction it seems that Jessie, left at this point, cannot herself rise out of the personal, as Rosa does, cannot move beyond the feeling that she has been treated unjustly, reductively, violently. She is in that way reminiscent of Gordimer's view of Olive Schreiner as motivated by her individual grievance. This may embody a consciousness of power relationships on the personal level, of course, but Gordimer also looks for the movement outward to the expressly public issues. When Rosa comprehends that "we succeeded in manoeuvering ourselves into the position their history books back home have had ready for us—him bitter," she is able not merely to forget what has taken place but to sublate it, that is, both integrate and transcend it. What seems to begin for her as treachery against her memories becomes an exposure of how societal conditions and education have undermined our relations with those we have known forever, lived and played with, and thought we understood, so that we end by returning and not recognizing one another.

It is not only the South African social system that causes these betrayals, lies, and secrets; as the author has said, that situation merely intensifies or magnifies what occurs anyway in life. Throughout her career Gordimer has set some of her stories outside her customary Africa; she has also written stories set in Africa that seem thematically indifferent to issues of race and politics, if not to class (which she always seems to perceive as integral to characters' awareness of their potential). These generally deal with relations within couples, and repeatedly they focus on the suppressed hostilities and disappointments that always threaten to undermine human happiness. It is as if she continually probes the possibility of escape, of pastoral bliss, of innocent happiness, and her characters cannot find these. In the social context this suggests that perfection is unattainable, because the private life is not perfect either, especially bourgeois dreams of happiness and success. It also suggests that one cannot blame all unhappiness on politics because we all share some kinds of human problems; however, it indicates that one cannot escape into the good life simply by ignoring politics. The political holds up the mirror to our own private lives.

The extent to which these motifs permeate Gordimer's view of human life in general and South African life in particular can be seen from two stories published some thirty years apart, "A Bit of Young Life" and "Crimes of Conscience." The first tells of a young mother who appears with her baby at a hotel in Durban, entrancing all the guests, including Ed, the worldly wise but tender-hearted traveling salesman who takes them in his care for more than two weeks as he and the other travelers ponder the mystery of her vacationing separate from the husband she never talks about. She and her baby are the object of solicitous attention from all the guests and staff, male and female, who are shocked and disappointed when she abruptly pays her bill and leaves. Two days later they learn the full story of her divorce scandal just breaking in the news, with the lurid information that she took her sister's boyfriend as her lover soon after the birth of the baby. Ed's gesture of caring is to send her two pictures of the child, from which she takes both "an odd comfort" and "a guilt sharper, a burden of duplicity heavier than she had felt for all the lies, the faithlessness, the cunning of her passion" (*Sel*, 68). Beneath the civil exterior of an ordinary woman seemingly bearing in stoic discretion some private dissatisfaction or unhappiness with which she refuses to burden anyone else has lain someone different, poised enough until having to confront her own betrayal of innocent and selfless trust. The story also suggests, of course, that even someone who appears on the outside to be conventionally decent and familiar can be capable of extraordinary behavior that casts away decency. This too has political ramifications: In "Something Out There," young Sergeant Chapman, the policeman who helps interrogate political prisoners, reflects on the unjust dangers of his job, not the least being that one's freed victims "often brought court cases against the State, you could find yourself standing there accused of assault, they tried to blacken your name in front of your wife, your mother and dad, who knew only your kindness and caresses" (SOT, 155).

In the later short story, "Crimes of Conscience" (published in the same volume as "Something Out There"), the subterranean lies undermine the public and private spheres simultaneously. Outside the South African court where a political trial is in progress, a man strikes up a casual conversation with a woman who has also been attending the sessions. Over coffee during the course of the trial, he tells her of his life away from his native South Africa, his growing political awareness, and his desire to become more involved; she, who obviously is politically involved and knowledgeable, gradually allows him into her interracial circle of friends, into her social life, and finally into her bed. During this time, however, she has remained guarded about her political convictions and activities, even about her reason for spending three months in prison rather than testifying against an acquaintance. Despite their romantic relationship, "she seemed to be waiting passionately to be given the words, the key. From him" (SOT, 63). He has certainly remained silent about the true impetus for his involvement with her, which is that he is a police agent trained to infiltrate the protest movement. Having settled on her as a likely target, he continues to sneak away to his now-barren apartment to type reports on her activities and connections, the most significant of which reside beyond the area of her life that she shares with him, that social environment in which she introduces him to black culture and the social freedoms of multiracial parties, and he reintroduces her to vacations and outdoor sports. Yet though they have become lovers, the covert truths leave a gap between them even in private moments, intimate moments. "But even now, when they lay in one another's arms, out of reach, undiscoverable to any investigation, out of scrutiny, she did not seem able to tell of the experience what there really was in her being, necessary to be told: why she risked, for whom and what she was committed." He at last "found a code of his own," which is nothing other than the truth: "I've been spying on you." That admission unleashes, of all improbable responses, her compassionate acceptance, as he "turned away before [her look] as a man does with a gun in his back. She shuffled across the bed on her haunches and took his head in her hands, holding him." The gesture is at once a mother's and a lover's, responding to his fearful desperation. One wonders, has she known or suspected, allowing him only so much closeness for her own sake, protecting herself until he at last gives in? Or has he manipulated her by an act of daring, risking her fury on the chance that his confession will win over her confidence, dismantle her last defense? Since the story ends with that gesture, we cannot know, and these too are ironic facts about such a situation, that even telling the truth may be deceptive, and the one spied upon may have become extremely adept at guardedly watching those who observe her, taking not even love or candor for granted.

It is the impact of public concerns on private lives that Gordimer so often writes about, and it is understandable that the impact is felt most strongly in the enforcement of secrecy, the sequestering of those attitudes and facts about race and commitments that cannot be shared even—perhaps most especially—between lovers. In the story entitled "Home," we can see the consequences of covert knowledge laid bare. Teresa is classified as colored (Xhosa and Javanese, in her case) under South African law, while her husband Nils is Swedish, a scientist working at a research institute. Their happy domesticity is interrupted by the arrest of her apolitical mother along with her sister and activist brother, all of them detained under a law effectively keeping them incommunicado. Glad when younger to escape her mother's obsessive protectiveness, Teresa now feels guilty because of her mother's suffering, growing ever more deeply involved with the case and with the political committee assisting detainees' families, then spending the night at other places to protect against also being caught up by the police, not even able to tell Nils where she will be.

As she becomes more secretive, she also becomes invigorated, changed by the energy of her new dedication; perceiving the flush of her new vitality, Nils convinces himself that she has a lover, perhaps someone in the movement, while feeling ashamed of himself for thus thinking ill of her. The story's narrative focus gradually switches to Nils, as Teresa spends more time out of sight and out of reach; his scope becomes ours, and his suspicions about her fidelity threaten to undercut our belief in her. As the evidence suggesting an affair builds in his mind, he becomes more certain that he will be returning to the austere, antiseptic white silence of his childhood home. When she comes back to him (like their sniffing dog, Nils "wanted and feared to get the scent of her betrayal"), she reveals that she has not and that she has forsaken him. She did not leave for another man. Instead, it is for her mother, whom she has visited against his express instruction that it is too dangerous. "She's all right. I knew you'd stop me if

I told you I was going" (*J*, 140). Rather than comforting him, however, this revelation confirms their separation, not in any clear physical or social sense but on the level of deep consciousness. Previously, each had found in the other what they needed in escaping their early life's confines, "the special closeness of a couple who belonged to nobody else" (*J*, 135). The fiction that she, a South African defined and determined as she is by the state, can make a separate peace, retire into the pastoral enclave of domestic harmony and belong to nobody else, is destroyed by the state's ability to deny that when they snatch her innocent sister and mother, that protective and cautious woman whose concerns were all domestic, in love of her children. "Perhaps there was no lover? He saw it was true that she had left him, but it was for them—for that house, the dark family of which he was not a member, her country, to which he did not belong" (*J*, 42). She has taken on a commitment, a belonging, which he cannot share despite his political sympathies, his desire to be supportive, and his willingness to undertake risks of his own on her behalf. The concluding sentence of the story ambiguously hints that "her country" may indeed be "the dark family"—her own and extended? Regardless, as contemplating Teresa's abandonment of him led Nils to thoughts of his own homeland, what clearly emerges through this experience is that South Africa is a country that he can leave behind, but she cannot.

In the dreadful balancing of obligations and passions, the great personal challenge may not be deciding what is right so much as it is understanding what to forgive. Max, the husband dead by suicide in *The Late Bourgeois World*, leaves behind him a trail of broken commitments. Some are personal: to his son, whose most recent birthday he forgot; to the wife he cheated on; and to the woman he slept with because it was easier than resisting ("She smothers you with her bloody great tits, you've got to fight your way out and that's the easiest way") (*LBW*, 64). Others are public: to the revolutionary movement he betrays in court after fifteen months in prison for an ineptly conceived and finally blundered bombing attempt; even to the authorities, whose case he sinks when he takes crucial papers with him in plunging his car off the bridge. He and his wife both knew that he was always desperate for "approval and admiration" (*LBW*, 64), which he could not get from her or from anyone else who counted; he was also so desperate to show his caring—that bourgeois gesture of principled vanity—that he would sacrifice self-respect and his comrades. Yet Max's mad, irresponsible, and undisciplined behavior must be measured against sober ineffectualness. "The liberal-minded whites whose protests, petitions, and outspokenness have achieved nothing remarked the inefficiency of the terrorists and the wasteful senselessness of their attempts. . . . *The madness of the brave is the wisdom of life.* . . . But why should the brave ones

among us be forced to be mad?" (*LBW,* 68). Gordimer is always hard—
some say hardest—on the grudging liberal reformists. Her writings direct
a powerful critique against those who disdain direct action but have nothing
more useful to offer—in Mehring's phrases, "the hopeful reasoning of the
impotence of your kind, of those who are powerless to establish their millennium" (*CN,* 154). She similarly exposes the hypocrisy of those who
sneer at their opponents in the power structure but glibly turn to them
when in need. That is to say, she shows us those who do not see themselves
by the light of their compromises and contradictions. Rosa Burger obtains
a passport through the help of Brandt Vermeulen, a sophisticated, cosmo-
politan member of the influential clique known as the Broederbond, to
whom she has access by virtue of her father's distinguished Afrikaner heritage. Hers is a minor, temporary compromise, less of integrity than rigidity, by contrast with Mehring's ex-lover, Antonia, who will flee the country
in the midst of a police investigation but not without turning to him, the
despised and powerful industrialist, for legal help; with his shrewdness, as
he listens to her on the telephone, "he could picture her saying to them, 'I
know someone, one of those tycoons who know how to do things.'" Even
as he knows their concept for him, he can take it along with his own contempt for them (*CN,* 41). Antonia's sexual duplicity, her adultery with him
(a man she is drawn to partly because he so confidently believes in what
she reviles), is a type of "covert action" that her politics imitates; it is also
"covered up" by that convenient secrecy that her political confederates and
absent husband accept as necessary.

The fissures in relationships that so interest Gordimer as a writer can be
discerned through such deceptions, self-deceptions, and acts of treachery.
These, in their mildest forms, such as Teresa's in "Home," only betoken
the independence, the integrity of each of us, the reality that even couples
may not succeed in totally obliterating one another's personality. In more
troubling manifestations, such as those discussed below, they express the
limits or failures of our ideals, idealizations, and cherished certainties. At
the deepest levels they mark the recurrent violations of honesty that include but are not limited to the political, those violations that we commit
in living our lives with one another and even with ourselves.

Some deceptions may be deliberate; others are unconscious, the result
of our own failures of perception or candid appraisal. Let us take, for a
story exemplifying the former, "Out of Season," in which the narrator
attends a luncheon given by a longtime friend now married to a much
younger husband, who is traveling out of the country.[3] Returning from the
bathroom, the narrator glances at the husband's most recent letter, from
which her friend had read at length during lunch, and notices that a sentence professing romantic yearning for her that had caused the other

woman to halt in attention-getting embarrassment is not actually in the letter. Without it, the communication seems amiable enough though not ardent. The friend's emendation reveals her insecurity, dissatisfaction, and compulsive need to justify her marriage.

One of Gordimer's most enigmatic stories, "Rags and Bones," addresses the cultivated secrets of life, incarcerated within a tin chest whose contents prove to hold a buried record of futility, of deceptions conscious and unconscious. Beryl Fels, an antique collector, has acquired the chest and inadvertently along with it, a cache of 307 letters, nine postcards, and numerous telegrams, all attesting to an illicit romance during the 1940s between a well-traveled and long-married male scientist (the correspondent) and a female author. The public danger in their relationship is attested to not only by the great care that he took to avoid discovery, evident from the letters, but also the recipient's proviso that the letters must be embargoed until twenty years after her death, then "presented to an appropriate library or archives" (SOT, 91). The fact that they instead end up being perused by a curious bargain hunter who obtained them by chance from a junk shop is the sort of ironic twist we might expect in a Melville story, but there are others. Fame has passed over both people, as has the life they might have lived together. Though the woman herself was presumably well known enough for the correspondent vigorously to refuse her attendance at one of his scientific presentations on the grounds that she would "be recognized at once by someone who's seen your photograph on your books, for God's sake!," it is he who ends up being preserved, at least in this minimal way, as an author before the public; her name proves to be unfamiliar to librarians and antiquarian book dealer alike, and a search of the library catalog shows that her titles had long since been removed to the inactive storehouse and presumably sold off with other unwanted volumes (SOT, 94). Her voice is quite lost; his endures in his various guises, as lover ("our great joy in each other's bodies and friendship"), literary critic ("you are one of the great names coming"), and social satirist ("why should you want to sit like some faculty wife [like mine, whose husband doesn't want to sleep with her and can't talk to her anymore] wearing an appropriate smile for the occasion, as she does a hat?)" (SOT, 94).

For the story's main character, the reader of those letters, the collection of one-way missives turns into something like an epistolary novel. Like us, she is drawn into the fictional world, at least temporarily accepting the characters' capacities for taking themselves seriously. We, and the narrator (who of course is fictional herself, or perhaps one should say, "herself"), take them seriously in other ways, oblivious to the reality of their nonexistence, their nonimportance in the scheme of things, and the dubious quality and achievement of the work that each supposedly has done.

So believing in them, we may be touched by the poignant irony that, as thoroughly forgotten as the female author's books are, the letter-writing scientist's career and even name seem totally submerged into an abyss. A distinguished scientist who works in this cautious lover's obvious field of expertise is unable to suggest who the globe-trotting (though not always sufficiently honored) scholar might have been. His "work" exists, in other words, through what she—rather than he—was known for, this literary artifact, a secret testimony of a private, illicit relationship.

Consequently, there is yet another irony, for their entire relationship has been hemmed in by his fears of public exposure and scandal, which was made probable by their individual fames. He graciously accepts her assurance that, despite minor disappointments over others' successes, he will one day win the Nobel Prize; he cautions her that not even transposed initials or code names in an intended book dedication can be permitted, because "separately, we are both people in the public eye; it's the price or the reward, God knows, of what we happen to be. Let the media scrabble and speculate over that" (SOT, 94). On the other hand, living this other way of life has given what they might otherwise not have had, a mystery and a passionate love story of some dramatic and erotic power, at least for those two participants, a literary entertainment they have created for themselves out of their lives and beyond their lives, for the reader they never anticipated.

Among its many meanings, this story satirizes the presumptions of the famous, who expect or pretend that their fame is both universal and lasting. More generally it sends up the capacity of us all for self-dramatizing, but especially the ability of those who lead semipublic lives and pretend that we are more public and more worthy of note than we are, indulging our capacity to take ourselves too seriously. That too is a layer of deception—self-deception added onto their trivial deception of the public.

Through the tale and the manner of its telling, furthermore, the teller becomes known in ways that only a reader can grasp. Even as this male figure of authority emerges through his own words as more "human" than the public man of knowledge, ideas, and attainments, so he consequentially appears radically culpable, weak, and cowardly. We evaluate him not only in light of the explicit, serious disloyalty to his wife but also in light of his implicit betrayal of his lover as he holds onto her through his earnest yet manipulative rhetoric, even as he timorously rejects all her efforts at more overtly satisfying her needs in the relationship. He reveals himself through these letters as petty, self-aggrandizing, self-protective, and consequently exploitive, a man whose flair for the dramatic verbal gesture covers his triviality. Still, because of the power of earnest words to command our attention, we may respond feelingly to the literary or personal familiarity of his rhetoric. Even with his self-serving duplicity exposed, he is at the same time also an engrossing though flawed writer and chronicler of a passionate obsession and romantic adventure.

The story itself depends on no particular geographical context. Because the letters sketch a relationship that extends through international travel, it suggests that the issues are universal rather than particular to a country. Read, however, in light of its author's South African context (so briefly evoked in a reference to an "old Cape lyre-backed chair" or perhaps the name of the principal character, Beryl Fels), emerge the deeper undertones of hypocrisy and posturing, taking oneself too seriously, clinging to appearances that are ultimately insignificant, repressive, or stifling, congratulating oneself and one another for defying the world's restrictive conventions while acceding glibly to conventionality and mutual self-deception about one's moral and intellectual stature.

This more epistemologically challenging situation, when people deceive themselves or allow themselves to be deceived about experiential reality, may be illustrated by "Face from Atlantis." In this story a group of sophisticated, successful refugees from Germany are thrilled by a chance meeting, a few years after the war, with one of the most lustrous of their old circle, the adored and charming Carlitta, whose radiant face has animated the group photos that, along with memories, seem to be the only reminders of a vibrant life before Hitler. To Eileen Brand, the young South African–born wife of one of them, who can know of that life only vicariously, Carlitta and her circle of young free-spirited socialists have sounded like the stuff of legends.

No longer the captivating teenager shown in those photographs but now in her forties, her unbecoming thinness letting the crinkles and sags of the years show, dressed drearily, and married to a figure out of stock comedy—a panama-hatted American Elks Club conventioneer named Edgar Hicks who lives on a farm and works for an agricultural machinery company—Carlitta presents Eileen with a challenge of visual interpretation. She responds to that challenge by telling her husband, "I don't think I should ever have known her," eliciting his rejoinder, "But Carlitta hasn't changed at all!" The persistence of his memory that he superimposes on the reality is not peculiar to him. One of their other friends, with equal determination, will insist not only on ignoring the physical changes but even integrating her choice of this mundane husband and commonplace life-style with the brilliant intellectual Continent-traveling coquette from their student days. To him she seems, "Still 'terrific.' Beautiful . . . She always chose the perverse, the impossible. She obviously adores him. Just like Carlitta."[5] Eileen, listening incredulously and with embarrassment, has seen through their self-deception or the triumph of their memory's tenacious hold over their perceptions but also sees through to something more paradoxical and much worse: The men are horribly right and do not know it. Carlitta (now a mother and a proudly unstylish rural housewife whose latest achievement was raising three hundred dollars in a high school bazaar) truly "had not changed *at all.*" Eileen had perceived earlier, in those revealing snapshots taken on a lost continent, an air of "arrogant" vanity and even manipulative contempt that had never been identified by those whom Carlitta's looks and manner had captivated. Now that attitude stands exposed as an essentially tawdry yet dominant element in her character to someone outside her charmed circle.

A more menacing version of unwitting deception can be found in "An Intruder." A frequently married, heavy-drinking, but urbane and high-living man charms, seduces, and then marries a very young woman, whom he treats with patronizing endearment, bestowing on her such epithets as "my little marmoset, my rabbit-nose, little teenage-doll" while introducing her to the varieties of sex "that she would not have guessed were lovemaking at all, and that he seemed to enjoy so much" (*Sel*, 380). When she is pregnant with James's first child, he tells her mother almost apologetically, "She's a little girl herself," indicating the tension in his quasi-incestuous eroticism, for "the signs of her womanhood saddened and delighted him" (*Sel*, 383). Jarring against his cooing amorous language reserved for her is the vitriol directed against his former wives, "that freckled bitch . . . Our Lady of the Plastic Peonies . . . those gorgons," with whom he would never "breed" (*Sel*, 382–83).

His compulsive heavy drinking does not seem to diminish his public charm, notwithstanding that he proves oblivious to anything said or done the night before. Marie's realization of that at last compels her to grow up, "as some people are said to turn white-haired overnight," following a mysterious incident in which she awakes to find every room but their bedroom hideously and obscenely vandalized, though nothing had been stolen and the apartment had been securely locked from the inside. As baffling as the crime seems to be, Marie has the disquieting notion that the devastation makes a kind of sense; for, "the mess spoke secretly, in the chaos there was a jeering pattern. . . . There was something related only to them in this arrangement without values of disrelated objects and substances; it was, after all, the components of their daily existence and its symbols" (*Sel*, 385). Like the would-be victim in the thriller, the pregnant young wife is trapped inside their new apartment and inside the marriage with the only suspect. Offering generic glances at conventions of the locked-room mystery and the horror story, Gordimer has created in the scene of spoliation a virtual allegory of the vulgar, ruined interior of the husband's mind and suggested as well the private and public disasters. "To her, evil had come out of the walls" (*Sel*, 386). That evil, we may suspect and she may come to believe, is the antidomestic and even misogynistic aggression with which James is suffused, for which his alcoholism and hatred for his previous wives, along with his oxymoronic view of her ("marmoset-angel"), are casual substitutes. Until that conclusive insight, when it becomes clear that no one could have gotten in and neither of them recalls anything about the previous night once they retired to bed, she has not grasped how well she really understands him. We perceive this, however, through a playful moment when they are newly married. She asks what he would call her if they got divorced and, outflanking his tender denial, Marie blushingly produces in a "vocabulary that was his" the phrase, "that sugar-tit tart"— another sexually vulgar oxymoron, expressing the hostility she has heard clearly in his language about the others he had once married (*Sel*, 382).

Like the female lover in "Something Out There," fearing they have not only been spied on but jeered at in their lovemaking, Marie feels as if "a malicious and wicked intruder . . . had scrawled contempt on the passionate rites of their intimacy" (*Sel*, 385). Like Mrs. Naas Klopper in the same novella, who learns that she had innocently entertained saboteurs under fraudulent names in "what she was always quietly aware of as her 'lovely home'" (*SOT*, 120), the young wife is horrified that someone has "smeared filth on the cozy contemporary home-making of the living room" (*Sel*, 386). Despite the private dimensions of this story, behind the husband's binges and his successful ability to live meagerly off the charm and social skills that make him useful to "the crude-speaking experts [who] felt themselves hampered in public relations by their South African inarticulateness" (*Sel*, 380), we may sense a farther-reaching critique of a society living beyond itself, superficially attractive and successful despite its obviously discernible crudity, facile in its disguises and self-deceptions. It is a society so intoxicated with its own sense of self that it does not know what it is doing or comprehend the brutality and violence of what it has done; it truly cannot remember for what it is responsible, wanting to believe instead that there must have been an intruder, an outside agitator that destroyed their secure home: "Are you sure there couldn't have been someone hiding in the flat when we came home, marmoset-baby?" (*Sel*, 386). James's Mr. Hyde–like repressed violence at last spills out all over the apartment, like a drunkard's vomit.

The connections between personal and public deceptions are explored in several of Gordimer's works, the most frequent pattern being a man who uses or takes advantage of a woman. It is here, in the diversity of outlooks and sympathies the author engages as she takes up the motif in various forms, that one can perhaps most clearly perceive how the concept interests her beyond the issues of political commitment. We have noted already that in "A City of the Dead, a City of the Living" the black woman betrays the activist hidden in her home; in "Crimes of Conscience" it is the female activist who seems to give in to the police informer; the wanted political activist in "Safe Houses" (*Jump*) both risks himself and hides out during an affair with a bored and wealthy married woman, politically unengaged and disaffected from her own social circle, who is willing to take him for a well-traveled construction engineer, which is rather a respectable parody of his real function as a trained guerilla. In "Good Climate, Friendly Inhabitants" (*Selected Stories*), where the man hiding out is a con artist and petty criminal, rather than a political activist, menacingly living off the woman, she is protected from him at last by a clever black co-worker whose intelligence and sensitivity to her unmentioned situation have not effected the slightest change in her bigotry. Through these variations on a common theme, the author suggests the prevalence of this pattern within our dealings with one another.

"Some Are Born To Sweet Delight," set within the context of the wave of international terrorism of the late 1980s, takes up this motif while it unfolds the cruelty with which the innocent can be manipulated and sacrificed, "in some complicated vengeance for holy wars, land annexation, invasions, imprisonments, cross-border raids, territorial disputes, bombings, sinkings, kidnappings no one outside the initiated could understand" (*J*, 88). That summary from the third-person narrator expresses the exasperated befuddlement of a sensitive intelligence unwilling to accept cant and contorted justifications, confronting the horrifying discovery not only that anyone and everyone could be held culpable, but that anyone and everyone—the hundreds of passengers sent to their deaths on sabotaged airplanes—could be taken as suitable martyrs for someone else's cause, one of their number objectified into a vehicle (in this story, literally) for someone else's vengeance.

One of Gordimer's few stories based on a real event, it unfolds betrayals as it accumulates innocent victims, most directly Vera, the white South African girl courted by a dark-skinned immigrant rooming in her parent's home. Seduced and pregnant, she is flattered by the grand adventurous prospect of flying to meet her fiancé's family in the unidentified eastern land from which he comes; it is he who sends her and their unborn child to their deaths, along with everyone else on the airplane, by means of the bomb he himself hides in her luggage. At the end of the story we may understand why he has called himself Rad, a nom de guerre, as we learn; it is only one of a number of his aliases, but it neatly marks him as the radical, whose principal victim and unwitting accomplice carries the name meaning "true." She has been faithful and believed in him at face value, believing she has seen something like the real person behind the dark facade that speaks to her parents' prejudices. What she has missed comprehending, in the thrill of sensuality and surprised delight that this exotic foreigner wants to marry her, are the sudden mechanical efficiency and unsentimentality of his love-making and eventual proposal of marriage and also the detachment with which he deals with her in the presence of his fellow émigrés with whom he converses in a language she does not understand. She cannot recognize the signs that might suggest manipulativeness or ulterior motivation to someone more sophisticated, more suspicious; she also feels so culturally different from him that she attributes anything strange in his speech or behavior to his alien background. Though she is specifically a victim of the radical's reductive, dehumanizing ideological dissociation of sensibility, cultural separateness has contributed to her vulnerability.

Gordimer's most complex interweaving of deceptions and betrayals develops in her novel published in 1990, *My Son's Story*, which opens with a vertiginous announcement of the theme.

> How did I find out?
> I was deceiving him. (*MSS*, 3)

What the narrator in fact found out was that his father was having an affair. The boy, deceiving the father by playing hooky from school to see a movie, met him coming out of the movie with a female political activist who is obviously his lover and so uncovers a more momentous deception. During the course of the book, as the father perpetuates this transparent fraud against his family and risky disregard of political prudence, the son further deceives him by probing the experiences of the liaison; the daughter will hide from all of them her membership in a militant group and later her marriage; and the quiet, domestic mother will also keep secret her participation with the guerilla group until she is arrested, herself first betrayed by an unknown deceiver and then framed by the prosecution.

The father's political activities necessitate that he and his family live anyway with understood boundaries for concealment. His involvement with someone outside the marriage and (because he is classified as colored) with a white woman in particular further compartmentalizes his communications with them. His family's covert penetration of his covert relationship, however (their never spoken, never mutually acknowledged secret knowledge of his secret), adds another hidden level of meaning to his comings and goings and to their most innocent-seeming communications with one another. His father's casual mealtime question about schoolwork at the home supper table after the movie incident establishes "complicity between us," the son records (*MSS*, 31). Much later, when the father rhetorically asks, as he agitatedly tries to help his wife's legal defense, "Would I lie to you?" the son is astounded that he and his mother accept the question at its ingenuous surface value, and "Neither of us affirms, yes, yes, and yes again" (*MSS*, 251).

His question reminds us how language exposes character along with thought. During a crucial scene of *My Son's Story*, Sonny addresses the crowd assembled for a grave-side political demonstration. In his speech, which builds on factual observations but never falls into a mere catalogue of facts, Sonny strips away the fraud preserved in the rulers' language (which has for instance designated the entities known as 'tribal home-lands'); he decries the plight of people "sent away after the day's work to urban rubbish heaps like this and to rural settlement slums in areas of our country given tribal names and called 'foreign states'" (*MSS*, 112–13). His own rhetorical qualities are noted at the time by his lover as indicative of his complete belief in his own integrity. "If he used the vocabulary of pol-itics because certain words and phrases were codes everybody understood . . . Sonny did not adopt the usual mannerisms the vocabulary pro-duces. . . . Watching Sonny, listening to Sonny, she felt at last she could define sincerity, also—it was never speaking from *an idea of oneself*." By contrast, he finds himself stymied during party infighting by an "orator" stuffed full with "an idea of" himself, whose stream of bromides happens to tumble out in support of the position that Sonny himself wants to take. Knowing the man's courageous past, Sonny hears this pompous self-revelation of vanity as embarrassing. Given an intellectual scrupulousness that exceeds his private integrity, Sonny cannot bring himself to advocate the same choice because it has been espoused with what everyone must hear as cant. Feeling committed to "plain speech, plain words," Sonny re-mains silent.

Though that choice allows him to retain personal integrity within the ideological dispute, it merely contributes to his further loss of influence. Unlike Hillela, he sets limits to his commitments, even though those limits are more determined by aesthetics than ethics. As an unidentified narrative voice (perhaps his son's) remarks, "A movement cannot be run by fastidious abstention" (*MSS*, 192). Sonny will be elbowed to the "backroom, useful for writing statements that appeared or were spoken under the names of the venerable, or for tidying up the vocabulary of the rising stars" (*MSS*, 263). In the urgency of political need created by the repressive State-of-Emergency laws, he becomes reduced, politically, to a useful style. Sonny's fastidiousness is the occupational hazard of the schoolteacher and Shake-speare devotee, his head filled with quotations whose persistent recall he comes to resent. "In a schoolteacher's safe small life, aphorisms summed up so pleasingly dangers that were never going to have to be lived. There is no elegance in the actuality—the distress of calumny and self-betrayal, difficult to disentangle" (*MSS*, 190).

Not even the reader is safe from these concealments and betrayals of confidence. On the penultimate page the principal narrator of the book, the son, admits about the narrative puzzle of such scenes as those intimately describing Sonny's sexual relations with both his wife and his lover, "I've imagined, out of their deception, . . . what others would be doing, saying and feeling in the gaps between my witness. All the details about Sonny and his women?—oh, those I've taken from the women I've known" (*MSS*, 276). The book ends with another challenging, enigmatic admission: "I am a writer and this is my first book—that I can never publish" (*MSS*, 277). What the real author, Gordimer, has done with this conclusion is to implicate us as well, both as people who have been deceived by someone's representation of truth and as people who have been prying into secrets, reading that which was "not for publication" (to quote the title of one of Gordimer's earlier stories and collections). If the title of this book implies that it has been published by one of the parents (presumably the father, a teacher proud of his own rhetorical skills who named his son "Will" after Shakespeare), then we must add yet another layer of duplicity and ambiguity in the recognition that it indeed is a "story," and a story of as well as by the son, with whatever level of presumptive truth we want to assign to that status. Despite a surface narrative compelling and plausible, this novel continually undermines our belief in authority and our acceptance of appearances. It repeatedly and richly explores not only for us but with us the consequences of our aparthood from one another in the body politic and in our private associations, "these incredible layers of concealment." As its raw tensions and ruptures are exposed, this book reminds us yet again that the concealments within the home and family are at once source and symbol of all others. In the final chapter we will examine Gordimer's treatment of those regions of conflict so misleadingly termed "domestic."

CHAPTER SIX

WHERE ONE MAKES A LIFE

 In the end, we return to earliest, deepest experiences, the shaping we undergo because of where we live and those we live among—home and family. Comprising the most obvious and ever-present facts of our lives, they also cover the experiences most anxiously concealed. No wonder that among the cornerstones of apartheid have been laws governing where people could live or had to live and to whom they were related or could be related through the creation of Bantustans as "tribal homelands," the Group Areas Act mandating residential segregation, the Population Registration Act dividing people into supposed racial categories, and the Prohibition of Mixed Marriages Act. In such legal constructs we perceive clearly how this particular patriarchy tries to lay a foundation for making a castle, even a fortress, of "a man's home," a white man's home where the black Africans keep to their place.

Gordimer, a white African, has probed repeatedly the double bind of the need to break free of the parental home and the need to find a place where one can be at home.[1] These needs entail tensions with parents and other family members that do not simply stand for but imitate the tensions also experienced with the pre-existing social and political structures within which we all live. For *home* also means *homeland,* and *family* means all those whom we identify as our kin.

The stirrings of sensuality, ruptures in the lines of communication, deceptions, and betrayals such as we have examined in the preceding chapters all occur with the most disturbing ramifications within the places where we live and the people we live with daily. These mean the most and last the longest. The author seems to have realized from the first that, as privately as tensions may be generated and experienced there, their deep political ramifications relate to our lives in society. That her concerns with these issues have not diminished in importance over the years may be seen through a glance at recent titles such as "My Father Leaves Home," "Home" and "Safe Houses" (all in *Jump*), "Letter from His Father," *Burger's Daughter*, and *My Son's Story*.

When, in Gordimer's first novel, Helen attempts to develop her friendship with her African classmate, she discovers the oppressive impoverished conditions in which Mary Seswayo lives. Moved to private philanthropy, she wants to provide a room in her mother's home in which Mary can study. Helen believes it would afford the young woman a place isolated enough from the raw struggle to subsist, a struggle that appears inescapable in her home location. Removed from the practical social conditions of black subsistence in an exploitive racist society, Mary could properly bend her mind (Helen thinks) to the more abstract idealizations she is being taught at the university, "the structure of the English novel, the meaning of meaning" (*LD*, 187). As naive as it is well intentioned, Helen's idea cannot overcome her mother's personal and social attitudes. Mary grasps this generational split and accepts that her liberal friend would have made such an accommodation in her own home. Much as Toby in *A World of Strangers* finds nothing odd about sharing eating and sleeping quarters with black men, regardless of whether he is in their homes or he in theirs, Helen and Mary could share a home if they were merely two private individuals. Yet both will have to realize that ameliorism is inadequate; indeed, it is worse, because it erects a barrier to consciousness. Helen does not want to see what the connection is between the life of her friend—past as well as future—and the life of the other black people with whom she lives in the present. Removing her from that is a way of abstracting her from it, in all senses of that word.

The notion of a white person trying unsuccessfully to make a place for a black person in a white home is suggestive of Helen's political angle of vision in which the country itself seems to be a "white" country.[2] The marginalized place of Mary, one of the few black characters in the book, indicates how the black majority appears only on the fringe of white consciousness. Furthermore, when one individual does penetrate closer to the center, as an exception, it may be somebody singled out as exceptional, one of the "worthies." Mary, for instance, because she is a university student, can be thought of as "just like us."

The mirror image of Helen's plan for Mary occurs in *July's People*. There, the black former servant, motivated by an instinctive sense of personal responsibility to some particular acquaintances in distress, offers a home to his once-affluent former masters, with somewhat greater success.

To the degree that it is his home, July is able to proffer space for them. To the degree that the local chief oversees all, they are able to stay only by the grace of his higher authority, which takes into account what they can offer in knowledge (the whites' form of productive labor here), as well as what the consequences might be of keeping them, depending on the state of things with a central government facing revolution inside and hostilities at its borders.

Their remaining in the village also entails that (unlike Mary, were she allowed to move into the Shaw house) they move down in the social and technological structure. For them, life becomes harder, devoid of accustomed comforts and pleasures, more primitive. They were accustomed to being in power, imagining themselves and their kind as central; the non-white South Africans had seemed marginal presences to be dealt with. Now, they themselves are outsiders, clearly in the minority, without political or economic power; they lack transportation (because their vehicle is no longer functioning or within their control) and the means of self-defense (because the theft of their gun demonstrates that they are now vulnerable to crime and without recourse, even as it removes from them their only weapon, taken by a black man for himself when he goes to fight). As powerless and marginalized as black people have been in the dominant white culture, the Smaleses are seen analogously by the current powers (July and the chief) principally as problems to be contained. This novel also seems to raise questions about what place there might be for a white African in an undeveloped and still essentially colonial and feudal African sociopolitical system and what it would be like for white people under that system, which itself is the by-product of years of white rule and suppression of black majority interests.

A Guest of Honour, set in a realistically depicted but imaginary African country, seems to pose that question in the context of black self-rule still dependent on white expertise and still fettered to a colonial system both corrupting and corrupt. Bray, having spent years in the country as a benevolent colonial administrator, is the guest in the title; unlike Toby in A World of Strangers, he is not merely an outsider, but one involved with and even committed to the country, knowledgeable about its economic and cultural history as well as needs, intimate enough with its current politics as they have developed through the process to nationhood so that he is caught in the midst of personal and ideological rivalries. He is, one can say, more fully enmeshed in the workings of the country than most inhabitants. Notwithstanding, he remains in a sense simply a guest.

The bitterly ironic circumstances of his murder toward the end of the novel make clear why this is so. The president whom Bray had befriended in the past authorizes white mercenaries to suppress a miners' strike threatening the national economy and (more importantly) his own power. The revolt occurs in a region Bray has been involved with for twenty years, where he knows well the inhabitants and language. While attempting to get his lover out of the country, Bray is caught in an ambush set for fleeing mercenaries by black workers who originate from another area and happen not to know him but see him merely as another white man; for them, a white man here must be a mercenary. At the terrible moment of his attack he tries to speak to them in the local language, in which he has long been totally fluent, "but he did not know a word, not a word of it" (*GH*, 469). He cannot call upon it in an emergency because it is not indeed his native tongue. An honored guest he may be, not an interloper or exploiter, but he is not a native.

These works develop tensions over the sense of home along racial lines. We recall that in the recent "Keeping Fit," in which the jogger is pulled to safety in a black family's shack, the racial connection with economic class is made manifest. "Safe Houses" (also in *Jump*) constructs two antithetical environments whose differences are founded on issues of privilege and commitment not directly linked to race but rather to socio-economic place. The man known in the story as "Harry" is a white political activist who had come back home to South Africa legally, lured by the promise of general amnesty, but now is a wanted man, hiding incognito among the crowds of Johannesburg during the group trial of his confederates. The daily news stories of the trial constantly describe his past illegal activities and mention his other aliases. On the lam, he moves from one safe house to another, now sharing a room with a plumber's three children in a bed temporarily vacated by a fourth, then imprudently seeking an old acquaintance in too small a town; there he hides in an outbuilding "in the company of a discarded sewing machine, stained mattresses and mouse droppings" for three days when, venturing out, he is arrested and sent back to Johannesburg and prison.

During his days of relative liberty in the city, he meets and becomes the lover of a wealthy, attractive, and sensuous woman whose husband is away on business. He invents for himself a profession, an ex-wife, and a pediatrician daughter. She in turn may have also invented a pseudonym, "Sylvie" (handily chosen, he notices, after her street's name); she too has reasons to hide her real name and seems to derive her identity more from where she lives than who she is. He even imagines telephoning, asking for Sylvie, and hearing the husband's voice tell him no one by that name lives there.

Their time together they spend at her lavish home in a tree-sheltered suburban neighborhood. Guarded by "pillared entrances in white battlements topped with black iron spikes," with "wide polished wooden gates" that open electronically when one conveys the right identification through the intercom, it abounds with lawns, terraces, swimming pool, cabana, and servants attending to them all (*J*, 189). On his last visit there—her husband is returning the next day—he realizes that he feels "safe, this night, that no one would know, ever, that he was here" (*J*, 207). As she had ingenuously remarked during their first meeting, "That's one thing about Johannesburg, isn't it, you can hide yourself in trees" (*J*, 187). They rarely discuss politics, not only because he would not risk raising the subject but also because she would not either. However, on one occasion, explaining her feelings about urban life, she makes clear that "racism" does not even begin to define her social thinking, virtually aristocratic in its aloof acceptance of class divisions that seem to date back to the Great Chain of Being. "They're unreal to me. I don't just mean because most of them are black. That's obvious, that we have nothing in common. I wish them well, they ought to have a better life . . . conditions. . . . I suppose it's good that things are changing for them . . . but I'm not involved, how could I be, we give money for their schools and housing and so on—my husband's firm does, like everybody else. . . . But the others—what have I in common with those whites, either. . . . I don't count in their life, and they don't count in mine" (*J*, 198). Her Olympian fastidiousness is not limited to blacks and most classes of whites but extends even to her husband, who has recently called from Australia. All she could think about as he spoke, she tells Harry, "was how when we're alone in here at night he never closes the bathroom door while he pees. I hear him, like a horse letting go in the street. . . . And sometimes there's a loud fart as well" (*J*, 202). Though she is satisfactorily "physical" during sex (as Harry remarks), she would prefer to close the door on other physical functions, much as she closes the gates on other peoples. Reflecting from his prison cell later, he thought that she probably would never know who he was, despite the extensive press coverage of his arrest and the trial, well illustrated with photographs of him. He recalls, "There were no newspapers to be seen around her house, that house where she thought herself safe among the trees, safe from the threat of him and his kind, safe from the present" (*J*, 209).

He does represent something of a threat as a guerrilla: "Sometimes pulling down," as Harry, the putative construction engineer, has told Sylvie in wryly describing his work, "Preparing to rebuild. Destroying old structures" (*J*, 191). It may be that he and his kind are also threats because they can make their safe houses anywhere, as the poor do, adults and children cramped together four to a room or amid old mattresses and mouse droppings. Instead of saying, "I'm not involved, how could I be" (which is a statement, not a question), they imply that they could not and would not avoid involvement and do not admit that there are classes of people who don't count in their lives, who are unreal.

These two people have met casually in the democracy of a Johannesburg municipal bus (her car would not start); they have formed their erotic alliance first through the primal equalizing medium of water, in her swimming pool where, wearing bathing suits, they are virtually stripped of clothing's social markers; and they have completed it by allowing themselves to experience together the passions of sexual gratification that all of us might share equally and that depend on no categories of race, gender, or class. That Sylvie imagines she has nothing in common with the rest of humanity is profoundly ironic. Perhaps her safe house, fortresslike, keeps out more than she realizes.

The cost, at times, may be too great even for people like Sylvie. The allegorical "Once Upon a Time" (also from *Jump*), a macabre response to the notion of writing a children's story, is set in just such a house and neighborhood, defended by gates and intercom, finally made especially secure by vicious toothed razor wire. It is that last obstacle that proves too tempting a challenge to the fanciful daring of the little boy the husband and wife and servants have wanted to protect, as if the barriers against intrusions from the outside will at last dare and destroy those not content simply to guard themselves against others.

Another story from the same volume, "The Ultimate Safari," perhaps the most poignant work Gordimer has ever written, confronts us with the homelessness of the dispossessed. Though it is specifically about the miseries of Mozambique, not South Africa, and does not deal with an exclusively African issue, one can see its relevance also to the displacements of people that have occurred in her country when populations are "resettled" into dreadful ostensible "tribal homelands" from which they (allegedly) originally derive. It also touches a nerve for South African readers because of South Africa's history of raids into Mozambique against ANC bases, its possible complicity in the mysterious crash in 1986 of the plane carrying President Samora Machel of Mozambique, and its widely alleged support for the RENAMO rebels against Mozambique's FRELIMO government. These particular refugees, we can feel, undergo their miseries because of South African government actions. More broadly, the story explores the ravages visited upon families driven from their homes by famine and war and offered no new homes but mired for years in temporary quarters as refugees. It is, we bitterly recognize, a story of too many places.

Narrated by a young girl who has had to flee on foot with her mother (now disappeared), brother, baby brother, grandfather (lost, presumed dead), and grandmother, the story takes them from their home, where they are caught in the civil war, on a trek with others in flight through the game preserve of the Kruger National Park, along South Africa's northeastern border with Mozambique, and finally into South Africa. There, though they live for years in a tent amid the poverty of a refugee camp, they are still tolerated by the local people, who surprisingly speak their language. Her grandmother has explained, "Long ago, in the time of our fathers, there was no fence that kills you, there was no Kruger Park between them and us, we were the same people under our own king, right from our village we left to this place we've come to" (J, 44). So they have been (at least) doubly dispossessed of their home, once generations ago when the white men carved up their lands, and now. The white woman who comes to film them interviews the grandmother and granddaughter, thus eliciting from them the differing opinions of the two generations, the one stoic but devoid of hopes or dreams, attention focused simply on the bitter struggle to keep these children alive, the other touchingly still grasping her youthful dreams. Asked, "what do you hope for the future," the older woman responds, "Nothing. I'm here." She has the familiar universal desires for the children "to learn so that they can get good jobs and money." When asked if she hopes to "go home" to Mozambique after the war, however, the grandmother steelily replies to her interviewer's prodding, "I will not go back. . . . There is nothing. No home." To the narrator this is fathomless, for she intends to return just as she came; "our mother may be waiting for us. And maybe when we left our grandfather, he was only left behind, he found his way somehow, slowly, through the Kruger Park, and he'll be there. They'll be home, and I'll remember them" (J, 46). The grandmother hopes beyond the present dismal reality to these children's futures as adults, no matter how early adulthood might have to come in their lives or how long they might have to wait. In contrast, the young girl longs for that which is even less possible—to go home again, not merely back to a place, but to a family that is in fact broken irreparably and to a childhood irrecoverably lost. Her concluding thought, "and I'll remember them," pleads to defy time. It asks, even as it pledges, not only that her memory will hold them ever as they were, but that they too will be unchanged, as if all could endure untouched by years or experience—a child's fantasy, a child's will, tenaciously surviving.

The slogan *Mayibuye* ("Come back, Africa") seems to underlie this story, though more deeply submerged than in the work about which the author invoked it, *The Conservationist.* In that novel, home begins to have different meanings: Mehring's flat, where he spends so little time that we can scarcely recall that he lives in Johannesburg; the farm domicile, in which Mehring is never settled, and which he never finishes into a home, despite his many plans; and the land, of which he becomes enamored, an unexpected development that complicates his original plans for it as an erotic getaway, "a place to bring a woman" (CN, 43). He takes the land not only as something to look at but also as something to be at home in and on, received by.

Antonia, for all her faults, spots this in his attitude, though her grasp of it may be too glib, her cynical dismissal too insensitive, not to his feelings but to the reality that is there in the land itself: "Mother it and husband it and lover it. . . . I'll bet you'll end up wanting to be buried there" (CN, 167). Lying down on it, he makes it into his bedroom, his maternal source (from which he emerges, in whose mud he sinks, into whose soil he plans eventually returning, like the buried and reburied African), and his only mistress during the course of the book itself. As a "conservationist" he is equally a possessive lover: "I don't have anyone hanging around here, thank God, if you walk about this place on your own, . . . birds and animals—everything accepts you. But if you have people tramping all over the place—." Thank God: like a new Adam in his own mind, Mehring believes he possesses this land he has paid for, as solely his, granted by the God of wealth.

This is not a disinterested love of nature, however; he seems to have eyes only for what nature produces on his property. Productivity in this case is an indulgence, for he does not maintain the land to be productive: "Mehring was not a farmer" (CN, 20). Capitalist though he is, he does not exploit the land; yet neither is he willing to let it serve the needs of the struggling people who live all around what has become his private yard. His foreman thinks, "He and his son with woman's hair came and went away, leaving nothing, taking nothing; the farmhouse was empty" (CN, 164). Not wanting to make money off of the land, he takes pleasure in his possession as a form of capitalist lust in which wealth, sex, and land are all part of his holdings. Mehring's enthusiasm for the variety of burgeoning nature equates with the voraciousness of his sexual fantasizing, as if the earth itself becomes another outlet for his appetite. What Mehring seems most to enjoy is the constant, changing fertility of the place. He has purchased his land the way Antonia recalls he has said he sometimes likes to pay women for sex, because he enjoys thinking, "She's doing this because I've paid her; she has to." He also wants to make the purchased land respond to his pleasure; for example, he pays a large sum for two imported chestnut trees he plants there, though they are not native to Africa and their survival is doubtful. As imprudent as it seems, it is not mere folly. Rather, it is a response to a deeper, larger impulse, a response to a mythic urge. In paying for it, as Antonia recognizes, "You've bought what's not for sale: the final big deal. The rains will come in their own time, etcetera. The passing seasons" (CN, 167–68). Mehring has beggared Gatsby.

Near the end of the novel, in a passage building toward his panic attack, Mehring sees a man—perhaps (he thinks) a thug, a police agent, or a mine detective, "same breed"—observing him and the woman to whom he has impulsively given a ride. At her behest, they have stopped for an impromptu suburban picnic amid the leftovers of the land's merchandising, the mine dumps and the former eucalyptus plantations. The stranger responds to Mehring's furious, frantic challenges by warning him, "It's not safe here. . . . They find you people here, they rob you. . . . They leave you naked. You won't have nothing" (*CN*, 249). We cannot certainly say what of this is supposedly real and what hallucinatory, but the message delivered by this mysterious figure threatens exactly what Antonia has taunted Mehring with in historical terms: "That bit of paper you bought yourself from the deeds office isn't going to be valid for as long as another generation. It'll be worth about as much as those our grandfathers gave the blacks when they took the land from them. The blacks will tear up your bit of paper" (*CN*, 168). Once, he could even joke sardonically, superiorly to her, "I'm planting European chestnuts for the blacks to use as firewood after they've taken over" (*CN*, 210). Now, in a no-man's-land with a woman whose wants and intentions he cannot fathom, his vulnerability grabs him, with the possibilities of humiliation and death. His secrets will be revealed; even his well-guarded public integrity will be taken from him, along with everything else. The scene ends in an imagined assault that recalls the killing of Bray near the end of Gordimer's previous novel, *A Guest of Honour*: A large white man set upon by mob of blacks, pulled down (they will "bring him down to them," as Mehring's hierarchical language puts it). Mehring in fact is not killed, though many readers have concluded otherwise from his frenzied hallucination. Instead, what he has experienced is the inevitable death of his claim on the land he purchased but does not possess.

"You won't have nothing." Mehring's empty future, foretold here with regard to property, suggests a connection with his familial future as well. When Antonia grandly evokes the biblical "handed down to your kids, and your children's children," Mehring reminds her, "I've only got one" (*CN*, 168). That one, disaffected and distant, perhaps gay, sufficiently opposed to the compulsory military service that one can easily imagine him joining the many others of his generation who emigrated rather than be conscripted, shows no interest in possessing this place, which he traverses on the edge of manhood with thoughts only of the sites he recollects. He comes and goes away, as Jacobus noted, leaving nothing, taking nothing. In his father's life, too, he tries to take nothing material ("Don't send an air ticket or the train-fare. I'll hitch" [*CN*, 70]), and he leaves nothing experiential except tension and unarticulated disappointments.

Early in the novel Mehring receives a visit from the neighboring Afrikaner family, come to ask for a favor. The talking is done by "old de Beer,"
who has arrived with his extended family, the son, the daughter-in-law,
their child, and the daughter-in-law's sister, a family grouping strikingly
in contrast to Mehring's solitariness, broken family, and secondhand home.
Looking admiringly at old de Beer's sturdy confidence, seeing how "the
retaining wall of belly and bunch of balls part the thighs majestically,"
Mehring thinks envyingly, "Oh, to wear your manhood, fatherhood like
that, eh, stud and authority" (CN, 47). Under this patriarchal authority, he
knows, the woman can meekly take only a soft drink, while the father-in-
law requests brandy in place of the proffered beer. A confident Afrikaner
farmer, de Beer exudes the image that he can lay claim to all. One family
heirloom in fact is "a kaffir doll they took from the chief's place, there when
they burned it during the war. . . . One of their dolls they used for magic.
It's not much left of it; there were feathers and little bags of rubbish tied
to it, but it's old now" (CN, 51). This is a rain queen fetish doll, a ritual
object in the Zulu religion, and it may get its revenge later in the novel
when rainstorms produce a flash flood through the area. At this time it has
become merely another one of the de Beer family souvenirs, despoiled by
their careless might.

Nonetheless, the old man still attests his interest in history, "The—
history—of—the—Afrikaner," he ponderously announces, as if this were
the most significant history to know. Living his life with such thoughtless
cultural egoism allows him to be settled here, while Mehring cannot feel
at home. Yet the reckless comfort of a de Beer is made at tremendous cost
to others, about which people like him remain indifferent. We may not be
surprised to find that the truck they have come to borrow is returned with
a broken light. The legacy symbolized in the disused, plundered ritual object taken from the burned camp is articulated in the name Zwelinzema,
suffering land, for which Rosa Burger's former friend, Baasie, is truly
named. It is borne also in Benoni, the name of the real town outside of
Johannesburg and northwest of Springs where Sonny and his family in My
Son's Story make their home. Sonny claims that someone has told him the
name is Hebrew for "son of sorrow." Actually the informant's Hebrew is
somewhat inaccurate; nevertheless, the error is close enough to the truth.
Benoni (if it does come from that language) should be translated, "son of
poverty." The conspicuously patriarchal culture is revealed to impoverish
its own sons, and if they identify with their land, they are left with the
legacy of suffering that names them. While one can say that history (and
not only South African history) could be understood as a story of "skin
and hair," one could as well claim that it is about land and kin.

Tensions where one lives go along with tensions with whom one lives;

grievances seem most potent when they occur in the most closed confines we know, the space of family relationships. Homes may become the sites in which families struggle in open or undeclared hostility over issues of authority, control, honesty, and selfhood, battling with one another through autocracy, manipulation, and deceit. The stresses between partners in married couples are pervasive, even when the families remain intact, as "My Father Leaves Home" reminds us, even though its title's tantalizing misdirection—the father left his native home, not the marital home. His daughter, the narrator, shows us enough of that marriage for us to ponder the other possibility, however. In "Sins of the Third Age" (*Something Out There*), as a long-married, seemingly perfectly matched couple renovate a retirement cottage in Europe, the husband becomes involved with a local woman, as if both his recognition of the passing years and the change of locale leads him also to a new, short-lived romance that will leave his marriage permanently damaged. The differences between the two women in *My Son's Story*, as we have seen, appear to Will's eyes as a difference between two homes, even between two images. His maternally tended home is dominated by the kitchen table, at which so much is discussed and avoided; at Hannah's, the central presence, visible as soon as one enters, is the bed on the floor, "close to the earth," as Will understands it, or as he contemptuously (and unfairly) sneers, "a whore's room" (*MSS*, 237).

The children, who also battle back, may become the territory over which the war is fought. So, Mehring and his ex-wife are at odds about Terry's future and character. When he finds a book about homosexuality in his son's backpack, Mehring is prepared to blame the boy's mother by reminding her that she accepted anal sex, as if she had passed on a predilection for it. In *A Guest of Honour*, Wentz's Jewish wife, quarreling with him over their daughter's behavior, has told him, "I blame myself. A Jewish father would have had some authority over his daughter. . . . He would have found somewhere better for his children to live than buried in this place. A Jew would have done better" (*GH*, 419). Ironically, Wentz had admired Wilhelm Reich's "sexual revolution as a break with authoritarianism in the father-dominated family," even during the rise of "Father Hitler and Father Stalin" (*GH*, 418). A further irony is that he is living in a country endangered by the conflict between Mweta, the president who was a radical in a previous generation, and his rival, Shinza, today's radical, who wants to overthrow this accomodationist and authoritarian relic of the past, this father figure.

The generational conflict, the civil war between the past and the future, is persistent. We have seen that Helen Shaw's attempt to reach beyond racialism is thwarted by her mother's conventionality, whereas Toby Hood's passage to South Africa oddly allows him to escape from his mother's obsessive antiapartheid activism. Years later, Rosa Burger will also resist—but only for a time—the burdens of parental commitments. In *Occasion for Loving,* Gordimer constructs a family background for Jessie unmistakably similar to her own: Jessie also is taken out of school at eleven because of an alleged heart ailment and prohibited physical activity; she too is used for emotional comfort by her mother, unhappily married to a European immigrant.[3] That background seems to contribute to Jessie's subsequent need to define an identity for herself and to her difficulty in doing so while her own past remains insufficiently grasped. Not that grasping it will necessarily yield a truth one wants to know. In "My First Two Women," for instance, the narrator's account of his relations with his mother and stepmother will lead to the truth about the former's abandonment of him; however, crushing disappointment and anger well up when the beloved stepmother "lovingly" reassures him, "We've really good friends, aren't we," eliciting both his unspoken recognition that good friends was indeed "all we were," and his concluding judgment," "I have never forgiven her for it."[4] Gordimer frequently probes the Oedipal tensions between father and son as paradigmatic of the issues that occur not only between parents and children but also between generations and between two different groups with different relationships to authority, the one possessing it by virtue of some unearned right of eminent domain, the other striving for it, seeing or reacting to all the reasons for not respecting the current possessors, for dispossessing them. To cite a recent example, the father's adultery in "A Journey" has inadvertently propelled his son at thirteen (traditional age of puberty) to assume paternal responsibilities. The son has known of the unhappiness between his parents, registering it through their mutual silences; now, after his mother has safely given birth in a European hospital, the rest of the family is returning to the father, who is working in Africa. The father, filled with regrets and guilt that we alone hear through his segment of the narration, feels determined to reconstitute his family life on the occasion of this birth. Seeing them in the airport, he mentally projects onto his son his own failures of responsibility ("an immature thirteen-year-old. . . . What's the matter with the boy? Why doesn't that boy stand by ready to lift off the baggage?"). The final tableau, however, gives him another insight: "But the boy is looking at him with the face of a man, and turns back to the woman as if she is his woman, and the baby his begetting" (*J,* 157–58).

As a writer, a daughter, and the mother of a daughter and a son, Gordimer also knows that the usual representation of the Oedipal crisis is flawed not only in its gendered specificity but in at least one other way about which an author would be particularly alert. She addresses this defect in "Letter from His Father," a story clever enough to be termed a tour de force but too deeply felt to be categorized as merely a virtuosic turn. It is a response to one of the most famous literary testaments in the chronicle of family relations, Kafka's "Letter to His Father," a searing exposure of the damage caused to a sensitive spirit and intellect by patriarchal autocracy, bourgeois vulgarity, and anti-intellectualism, as well as superficial Jewish religious observance devoid of spirit or ideas. Kafka's work, in turn, may be connected directly with another of Gordimer's texts, Sasha's letter to his parents read during his political trial in *A Sport of Nature*. In that document denouncing their ineffective liberalism, Sasha blames them and their generation for the violence then affecting white areas. As if sensing a connection between what he feels to be their (especially his mother's) stifling of him and the white suppression of black freedom, he asserts, "It's the whites who have killed their own children" (*SN*, 373).

What Gordimer recognizes from her angle of vision is that the "truth" of any narrative (even the Oedipal one) depends on who is telling it. Her short story takes the form of a posthumous letter from Hermann Kafka, the father. First published in 1983 and reprinted in *Something Out There* at a time when she was more actively exploring the aesthetic values of multiple narrators, Gordimer may well have perceived that one defect of Kafka's letter (published posthumously), like all such exercises, is that it gives us, for the most part, only one party's angle of vision and voice. In other works she will incorporate the viewpoints of two or more distinct characters in one story; here, cleverly, she gives us the viewpoint of the one character who could only be silent and unaware while Franz Kafka told his story, supposedly to his father but, as it turned out instead, to the world.

Or almost silent. Gordimer's Hermann Kafka specifically explains, "I am writing this letter because you tried to write it for me. *You would take even that away from your father*" (*SOT*, 54). Kafka had written in his letter an imagined reply from his father. "You take the words out of my mouth," Hermann now objects. In letting him speak for himself (obviously yet another level of ventriloquism but still a rejoinder from his angle of vision), Gordimer fulfills one of the literary roles she particularly has undertaken in her stories, to give a voice to those whose voices we usually do not hear because their race or level of education deprives them of attention or of access to the literate community. In taking the words out of his father's mouth ("You are there, quickly, with an answer, before I can be"), Kafka has abused both his talents and his father. He has failed in understanding and compassion to one who "hadn't much time for reading, working like a slave since I was a small boy" (*SOT*, 55).

In entering into this sympathetic and thoughtful engagement with Hermann Kafka, Gordimer may partly be coming to terms with her relationship with her uneducated, unintellectual father, whose personality she had found wanting and whose Jewish practice (nominal as it was) she did not share. More generally, she challenges a reader's sympathies in a way reminiscent of her treatment of Mehring, although the two cannot be equated. Not only describing but writing through his way of thinking, she allows the elder Kafka to defend his industriousness, his religious observance, and his enjoyment of life and also to criticize his self-pitying, self-centered, overly intellectualized famous child, who repressed all that his parents offered and eventually did himself out of life at too early an age.

In rebuttal to his son's implied complaint, "See what you did to me," the father responds, "Why did you act like that?" The father's letter rejects the son's attempt to posit the miseries of his life as imposed upon him by parental mismanagement, as somehow determined. Instead, he points to choices, to deliberate decisions to do or to suppress, to take only negative interpretations, and in so doing, the father insists that the son was an independent person. Despite the split between them, however, the father concludes by observing, "We've ended up as we always should have been, united" (SOT, 56). They are united in death, and they are united in fiction by this story making them into a family unit, seen as a whole with its fractures and pains from the other angle as well as the one we have known.

Hermann Kafka's supposed text shows him to be intelligent and observant despite his not being an intellectual. For instance, he spots the artist's imperialistic ego that wants to lay claim to all, to subsume all within its own domain, to impose its version of truth on the public consciousness. Appropriately for someone who can claim, "I know I'm no intellectual, but I knew how to live!," he protests on behalf of the living vitality that does not want to be so subsumed. He also protests, in the name of family decency, against the writer's shamelessness in exposing, complaining against, maligning them, as if they had no right to the privacy of their own lives. They have become, as anyone around a writer is liable to be, merely subject matter, and in this case, tendentiously portrayed; the son's text has also made them subject matter for all other people who will pry after them because of his fame.

The story addresses the effect on the writer's family of something they cannot control, the fact that the person connected to them is a writer, who by virtue of that compulsion may take the meanings of their lives out of their mouths. That Gordimer will turn in My Son's Story to another writer who does exactly this indicates the significance of the motif and the intractability of the ethical problem for a writer who sees the connection between origins and production.

The relationship between Will and Sonny repeats at a more complex intensity the split between Mehring and his son, Terry, regarding the tensions of sexuality. In the earlier book the father, proud of his own sexual profligacy, thinks of his stubborn, shy son still at boarding school (a son who he later finds is reading a book about the civil rights of homosexuals): "Terry—that is certain—had no woman in there, only masturbation and compassion" (*CN*, 97). But Will, narrating his and his father's story, proudly announces his women to us, even as he dares the taboos of violating the privacy of his father's sexual behavior. He does so with brash, exaggerated, and inappropriately hostile macho vulgarity, as if reacting to his father's compulsive sexual need for Hannah by supplanting it with his own sexuality, which manifests itself flippantly, in a dominant rather than dependant or even cooperative way. Though Hermann would not, Franz Kafka would be appalled. "I went down to Durban on the motorbike and picked up a girl on the beach the first day. It was easy. Some of the beaches are open to all of us now. So I've lived with a woman for six days, fucked her and slept in the same bed with her, and don't want ever to see her again" (*MSS*, 136). Sonny's relationship with Hannah seems balanced in male/female as well as private/public dynamics, although personally he "needs" her. Will differentiates himself by a verbal show of being controlling and powerful, using women and sex but doing so crudely, not seeming to need them or depend on them as his father had. It was the movement's recognition of Sonny's need for Hannah that marked him as unreliable, not willing to give up everything.

By announcing that "It's my time that's come, with women. My time that's coming with politics," Will does nonetheless implicitly acknowledge a connection that we can see as an inheritance from his father, although he will live it out differently, associating sex and politics (*MSS*, 276). His emphasis on time also implies that the personal struggle with his father is symbolic of the generational struggle between activist generations. This affirmation of his personal future is the closest Will can come as yet to the prophetic articulation of a new vision, a new generation. Sonny's is the one being supplanted. Although it was shaped out of moving, articulate rhetoric coming from the educated and thoughtful, from the ideologically committed and perceptive, it outlasted its effectiveness. The emerging generation is more manipulative, political in the worst sense, trying to be effective by making deals even with scoundrels. Those coming have seen through the previous generation of leaders, like Sonny. It has seen them as flawed, needy human beings with personal weaknesses, guilty of private treacheries, unreliable; therefore, it is prepared to discard them. So too his family has moved ahead, independent of him, each member leaving behind the patriarch, who still bears the name "Sonny." The daughter he named Baby is now a political activist with a militant group operating outside the country, free of that traditional structure, with a husband and baby of her own; his son, named for his own favorite author, is paradoxically both in rebellion against him and yet a writer, made so by him and against him.

Even his modest, domestic wife is now more than a political activist; she is a revolutionary and a globe-traveling exile, wanted by the South African police. The change in Aila as she reacts to Baby's pregnancy is something that Sonny actually identifies as being "brought to life . . . a new life coming out of the old one he left her buried in" (*MSS*, 170). When they visit Aila later in prison, they find an even more remarkable metamorphosis: "Through the familiar beauty there was a vivid strangeness. Boldly drawn. It was as if some chosen experience had seen in her, as a painter will in his subject, what she was, what was there to be discovered" (*MSS*, 230). So Aila has emerged as someone transformed, separate from what she was. We may even suspect that the mines and grenades she allows to be hidden at home express at a deep level the contained potential for explosive rebellion that has been latent inside her and that bursts forth not as something only violent but also liberating.

For a time, Sonny, still deeply involved in his affair with Hannah, had felt that the change in Aila, this rebirth, had allowed him to be "rid of Aila. Free" (*MSS*, 170). Later, with Hannah truly gone, both Sonny and Will understand that "Aila was gone, too," even before jumping bail and fleeing the country (*MSS*, 243). Both she and Hannah have gone on to new challenges and opportunities, Hannah to a major position with the United Nations High Commission for Refugees. Perhaps Aila and Baby, who have not had Hannah's opportunities for arguing sophisticated ideology or analyzing grand political strategy, take the most daring way accessible to them and thereby commit themselves to a seemingly old-fashioned, even anachronistic mode of political engagement—armed struggle. Still, all three women engage themselves with a wholeness of practical commitment and acceptance of militancy that carry them outside of Sonny's personal and tactical spheres. Their time with politics has come—the time of women.

Sonny's absence from home at the two moments of deepest personal crisis for his daughter and his wife (first, when Baby attempts suicide and second, when Aila is arrested) both occur because he is with Hannah. He has, in a sense, failed both of them for another woman, irresponsibly abandoning them even as he shares both passion and politics with his mistress; his political activity becomes a convenient cover for his leaving the house, as it did for Mehring's Antonia. Ironically, Aila is arrested for her revolutionary activity at just such a moment, so another crisis occurs that brings together significant elements contributing to Will's contempt for his father. To the women, including Hannah, the evidence is too clear that they cannot depend on Sonny personally. Hannah shocks Sonny by weeping when she learns of Aila's arrest, as if she has a bond of affection with his wife that he has not grasped. Later, contemplating the job offer, Hannah perceives the signs of Sonny's slip from political prestige and influence. Rather than sustain the conflict in the grip of psychological struggle, as the son does, they move in their own directions.

In these ways as well, the old structure has given way. What will replace it is not clear to Sonny or Hannah. As they discuss the impact of global political changes on South African possibilities, she hopes that "the new Left that's coming" will offer freedom that the old collapsing socialism could not bring, but Sonny shrewdly notes the threatening specter of "the return of the old nationalism" (MSS, 215). The dynamics of political structural change connects with that of family structural change: In a time of transition, it seems impossible to tell whether the reforming is going to produce something genuinely new or merely a return of the old. That indefiniteness is captured by the liminal situation of the narrator and main character, Will, who concludes the novel stating, "I am a writer and this is my first book—that I can never publish" (MSS, 277). He himself and his book are in an indeterminate state; he has an identity on paper, but it cannot yet be manifested publicly. If this is not politically allegorical, it is at least politically resonant.

As a writer and as someone sexually and politically aware, Will lives a divided life. Sex is his activism of the present, and politics his activism of the future; yet any writer is always actively engaged with the past. The past, including the literary past, is embedded in the language and tightly woven throughout this particular book. It is there as something else that the Shakespeare-obsessed Sonny has imparted to his son, Will; it is there also because the patterns of words, thoughts, and actions articulated by the literary tradition are inextricable from the mind of anyone who writes or speaks from the context of this culture. It is there because the writer's material is likely to be in some way a story coming from the store of past experience. One meaning of the ambiguous phrase "my son's story" is that it is the story written in the capacity of a son.

Gordimer knows, therefore, though Will may not, the literary (as well as psychological) origins of Will's contemptuous and obsessive confrontations with his father's sexual behavior. He forces himself to somewhat evasive admission of both parents' sexuality, but there are no evasions in confronting the physicality of his father's relationship with his mistress as well as his own sister's sexual relationship:

> They sleep in the same bed, but does he love her, after he's come from the other one? I never used to think about them—him, my mother—that way. I don't want to think about it now. (MSS, 46)

I wonder how he could go on doing it knowing he was so old—what's it? Over fifty—and some other man was also doing the same thing to his darling daughter.

Fucking his pudding-faced blond (pink blancmange like my mother used to make for us out of a packet when we were kids) while he ought to be dandling his grandchild on his knee. It's disgusting to think like this about him, I know, but he's the one who's brought it about. (*MSS*, 175–76)

It obviously derives psychologically from the writings of Freud, even the anxiety expressed in persistently calling the man who does all of this "Sonny" or "he," rarely "my father." Significantly, one point at which he is deliberately designated by consanguinity is in the concluding judgment, "What he did—my father—made me a writer. Do I have to thank him for that? Why couldn't I have been something else?" (*MSS*, 277). This narrator's literary attitude toward his subject seems inherited from another work with which we know the author is familiar, Kafka's "Letter to His Father."

Unlike Franz, whose destructive behavior was purely literary, however, Will does attempt to act out the Oedipal pattern. At one point, holding his father responsible for his mother's arrest, he really intends to kill him in the midst of his adulterous liaison (an urge somewhat reminiscent of Hamlet's regarding Claudius). What prevents him is that the lovers have gone out of town for their tryst, and when, frenzied, he runs from her cottage, he is nearly struck by the bullet shot at him from the main house, by those who have mistaken him (though it is in its way no mistake) for an intruder. Instead of a murderer or a dead man, he becomes a writer, also an intruder.

That is at least one way to think of a writer: as an intruder. For the writer not only shamelessly pries into and pitilessly pries open; the writer intrudes upon certain fictions, upon our unspoken, even our unrecognized thoughts, revealing the lies we have grown to take for granted, betraying the patterns and structures to which we have become so accustomed that we no longer notice them. These include the most basic as well as the deepest that we know, the patterns and structures shaping what we call home and who we call family. In doing so, the writer startles us into noticing, recognizing, being aware.

Will is still raw, though far from naive. His destructive impulse, motivated by vengeance as much as by justice, has nearly destroyed him prematurely. Drawn by sensuous experience and set in motion by a parent's perfidy (like his creator herself), he finds through art the way to attack his target, and though he may do so with a killer's steely disregard for all that the victim wants to preserve, he effects a response in which ruin gives way to creation. Named deliberately for England's paradigmatic writer, named coincidentally for that amoral trait that urges any writer onward, he must learn to fuse what his creator termed "the two presences within—creative self-absorption and conscionable awareness." His determination to do that is proclaimed in the sentence with which this study opened, a sentence declaring his prophetic will to be the writer who will write the book of freedom's struggle as he has lived it in his home and his South Africa.

To be an intruder is one of the revolutionary functions of the writer. The other is to be a prophet, a role which any realist will hold in tighter rein. Both are functions that Gordimer knows well, having practiced them so brilliantly during her remarkable career. Her two most recent books (*My Son's Story* and *Jump*) show her at the height of her artistic powers, mining physical, emotional, and social territory she has dwelt in since her days in Springs in the work that has taken her to Stockholm and the Nobel Prize. As this study has tried to show, she has explored not only the "inner history" (as Stephen Clingman demonstrated) of her own country but the inner experience of us all. To both, she has committed the rigors of art and moral judgment, with no illusions about the power of art to effect change, but still the conviction that speaking the truth, so far as one perceives it, is an obligation the artist, of all people, cannot shun. (It is this conviction that she has proclaimed repeatedly in defense of Salman Rushdie, still under threat of death for having published *The Satanic Verses*.) For although knowing the truth will not necessarily set one free, she seems to suspect there can be no personal or political freedom unless one tries to know and express truth. That quest may demand of one an honesty or candor not always appreciated. In her Nobel Prize speech, Gordimer professed that "the writer risks both the state's indictment of treason, and the liberation forces' complaint of lack of blind commitment."[5] With characteristic awareness of another allegiance to a higher claim on the artist, she affirms that the writer's language is both means and end, the instrument of liberation and the manifestation of it: "The writer is of service to humankind only insofar as the writer uses the word even against his or her own loyalties."

Gordimer also seems to believe that being of service to humankind is a worthy ambition even for an artist. For her, this seems to be the covenant and commandment we share with one another, answering our common human demand for justice, peace, freedom—large concepts and ones many artists and intellectuals of our time openly shun, some for the right reasons, some for the wrong ones. The character named Hillela is Gordimer's one protagonist who lives to witness the millennium (if not the messiah), the arrival of freedom to South Africa, and it is she who has committed herself to "the rainbow family." Hillela, who does not look to the past, obviously bears in her name the legacy of the great rabbi of the first century B.C.E., Hillel. Whether or not Gordimer herself has ever found them in her reading as an adult, Hillel's most famous aphorisms succinctly articulate those rhetorical questions that seem to absorb her characters amid the ethical contest of their own lives:

> If I am not for myself, who will be?
> If I am only for myself, what am I?
> If not now, when?[6]

Autonomy, connection, and commitment are the principles that Gordimer has explored repeatedly and with sustained energy and acuity. Underlying that exploration have been two moral imperatives to which her characters as well are answerable, both appropriately expressed by Hillel's great precepts, which shall stand here as the epigraph to this study:

> *What offends you, do not do to anyone else.*

> *In a place where no one behaves like a human being, strive to be human.*

NOTES

INTRODUCTION

1. Nancy Topping Bazin and Marilyn Dallman Seymour, eds., *Conversations with Nadine Gordimer* (Jackson: University Press of Mississippi, 1990), p. xiii. Hereafter, this work is cited as *Conversations*.

2. Nadine Gordimer, "The Essential Gesture," in Gordimer, *The Essential Gesture*, ed. Stephen Clingman (New York: Alfred A. Knopf, 1988), pp. 299–300.

3. Edmund Morris, Interview with Nadine Gordimer, *New York Times Book Review*, 7 June 1981, p. 26.

4. Robert F. Haugh, *Nadine Gordimer* (New York: Twayne, 1974).

5. John Cooke, *The Novels of Nadine Gordimer: Private Lives/Public Landscapes* (Baton Rouge: Louisiana State University Press, 1985).

6. Michael Wade, *Nadine Gordimer* (London: Evans, 1978).

7. Stephen Clingman, *The Novels of Nadine Gordimer* (London: Allen and Unwin, 1986). A revised edition with a new prologue was scheduled for publication by the University of Massachusetts Press late in 1992.

8. Nadine Gordimer, *The Essential Gesture: Writing, Politics and Places*, ed. and intro. Stephen Clingman (New York: Alfred A. Knopf, 1988).

9. Judie Newman, *Nadine Gordimer* (London: Routledge, 1988).

CHAPTER ONE: A WHITE WOMAN WRITING IN SOUTH AFRICA

1. Richard F. Teichgraeber III, "Cry for the Beloved Country" (interview), *Tulanian* (Summer 1987): 30.

2. Todd S. Burdum, "Dinkins and Gordimer Debate Race Relations," *New York Times*, 15 November 1991.

3. See, for instance, the interview with Miriam Berkley, *Publishers Weekly*, 10 April 1987, p. 81.

4. Nadine Gordimer, "Bennett Award Acceptance Speech, 1986," *Hudson Review* 40 (1987): 182.

5. Nadine Gordimer, John Dugard, and Richard Smith, *What Happened to "Burger's Daughter," or How South African Censorship Works* (Johannesburg: Taurus, 1980).

6. Gordimer, "The Essential Gesture," p. 287 and n.

7. Henry Kamm, "Writers, Meeting in Budapest, Warm to a Concept," *New York Times*, 22 June 1989, p. C21.

8. Gordimer, "Living in the Interregnum," in *The Essential Gesture*, p. 279; essay first published in 1982.

9. Beata Lipman, "Nadine Gordimer" (interview), in Lipman, *We Make Freedom: Women in South Africa* (London: Pandora Press, 1984), p. 109.

10. Gordimer, "Living in the Interregnum," p. 279.

11. Gordimer, "The Essential Gesture," p. 299.

12. Lipman, "Nadine Gordimer" (interview), p. 107.

13. Carol Sternhell, "Nadine Gordimer: Choosing to Be a White African" (interview), in *Conversations*, p. 276.

14. Gordimer, public discussion with Neil Lazarus, Brown University, Providence, R.I., Conference on the Future of the Novel, 30 April 1987.

15. Claudia Dreifus, "Nadine Gordimer: 'I've never left Africa'" (interview), *Progressive*, January 1992, pp. 30–31.

16. See, for instance, Cynthia Ozick, "Justice to Feminism," in *Art and Ardor* (New York: Alfred A. Knopf, 1983), pp. 261–90.

17. For instance, Jill Fritz-Piggott, "Stranger in a Strange Land," a review of *The Essential Gesture* in *The Women's Review of Books* 6 (February 1989): "Readers of Gordimer's fiction may be disappointed by the lack of any extended feminist argument in *The Essential Gesture*, and her exclusive use of the masculine pronoun may put them off" (p. 3).

18. Ibid.

19. Nadine Gordimer, "The Prison-House of Colonialism," in *An Olive Schreiner Reader: Writings on Women and South Africa*, ed. Carol Barash (London: Pandora Press, 1987), pp. 225–26. Originally printed as a review of Ruth First and Ann Scott's *Olive Schreiner, Times Literary Supplement*, 15 August 1980.

20. Jannika Hurwitt, "The Art of Fiction LXXVII: Nadine Gordimer" (interview), in *Conversations*, pp. 139–40.

21. Gordimer, "The Essential Gesture," p. 296.

22. Hurwitt, "The Art of Fiction" (interview), p. 129.

23. Ibid., p. 159.

24. Gordimer, "The Prison-House of Colonialism," p. 226.

25. Sternhell, "Nadine Gordimer" (interview), p. 278.

26. Gordimer, "The Prison-House of Colonialism," p. 225.

27. Hurwitt, "The Art of Fiction" (interview), p. 155. The first elision occurs in the published text.

28. Ibid., p. 154.

29. Gordimer, "Selecting My Stories," in *The Essential Gesture*, p. 113. Originally published as the introduction to her *Selected Stories* (London: Jonathan Cape, 1975).

30. Gordimer, "A Bolter and the Invincible Summer," in *The Essential Gesture*, p. 26.

31. Ibid., p. 27.

32. Hurwitt, "The Art of Fiction" (interview), pp. 153–54.

33. Sternhell, "Nadine Gordimer" (interview), pp. 275, 278.

34. Gordimer, "Selecting My Stories," p. 113.

35. I am relying on a partial text, published in *Poets and Writers Magazine* 20 (May/June 1992), pp. 19–24.

36. Nadine Gordimer, "Leaving School II," *London Magazine* 3 (1963), cited by Ethel W. Githii, in "Nadine Gordimer's *Selected Stories*," *Critique: Studies in Modern Fiction* 22 (1981).

37. Hurwitt, "The Art of Fiction" (interview), p. 139.
38. Ibid., p. 144.
39. Sternhell, "Nadine Gordimer" (interview), p. 278.
40. Hurwitt, "The Art of Fiction" (interview), p. 159.
41. Gordimer, "The Essential Gesture," p. 298.
42. Gordimer, "A Brilliant Bigot," review of Martin Rubin, *Sarah Gertrude Millin: A South African Life*, in *Times Literary Supplement*, 15 September 1978, p. 1012.
43. Lipman, "Nadine Gordimer" (interview), p. 108. Gordimer also cited the impact of Sinclair's book in Teichgraeber, "Cry for the Beloved Country," (interview), p. 30.
44. Gordimer, "Selecting My Stories," p. 113.
45. Sternhell, "Nadine Gordimer" (interview), p. 277.
46. Teichgraeber, "Cry for the Beloved Country" (interview), p. 30.
47. Lipman, *We Make Freedom*, p. 107.
48. Lipman, "Nadine Gordimer" (interview), pp. 106–7.
49. *Illustrated History of South Africa* (Pleasantville, N.Y.: Reader's Digest Association, 1988), p. 445.
50. See for instance the chronology in Bazin and Seymour, *Conversations*, xix, and the 1986 Junction Avenue Theatre Company interview titled "Nadine Gordimer," in that volume, p. 248.
51. Hurwitt, "The Art of Fiction" (interview), pp. 130–31.
52. Joseph Cohen, "Nadine Gordimer's Jewish Origins," *American Jewish Times Outlook* 57 (1992): 23.
53. Junction Avenue Theatre Company, "Nadine Gordimer" (interview), p. 248.
54. Cohen, "Nadine Gordimer's Jewish Origins," p. 23.
55. "Joe Slovo: Apartheid's Foremost White Opponent," *Jerusalem Report*, 17 October 1991, p. 49.
56. Hurwitt, "The Art of Fiction" (interview), p. 151.

CHAPTER TWO: OUT FROM SPRINGS

1. Nadine Gordimer and David Goldblatt, *Lifetimes: Under Apartheid* (New York: Alfred A. Knopf, 1986), p. 53. This and the other two accounts of photographs in this chapter are my own.
2. Hurwitt, "The Art of Fiction" (interview), p. 131.
3. Ibid., p. 132.
4. Cooke, *The Novels of Nadine Gordimer*, pp. 1–90, analyzes the theme of an independent daughter rebelling against a possessive mother in Gordimer's fiction, tracing it to the novelist's own experience.
5. Jill Fullerton-Smith, "Off the Page: Nadine Gordimer" (interview), in *Conversations*, p. 302.
6. Hurwitt, "The Art of Fiction" (interview), p. 135.
7. Gordimer, "A Bolter and the Invincible Summer," in *The Essential Gesture*, p. 21.
8. Cohen, "Nadine Gordimer's Jewish Origins," pp. 22–23.
9. Junction Avenue Theatre Company, "Nadine Gordimer" (interview), p. 248.
10. Hurwitt, "The Art of Fiction" (interview), p. 130.
11. Melvyn Bragg, "Nadine Gordimer: The Solitude of a White Writer" (interview), in *Conversations*, p. 75.
12. Junction Avenue Theatre Company, "Nadine Gordimer" (interview), pp. 249–52.
13. Gordimer and Goldblatt, *Lifetimes*, p. 91.
14. Here I obviously disagree with the thesis propounded by Cooke in *The Novels of Nadine Gordimer*, pp. 91–221. Cooke, noting (p. 93, esp. n. 5) the frequency with which Gordimer's early technique had been described as "photographic" argues that as her work has developed in complexity and in involvement with the public sphere of Africa, her writing has become more "painterly."

15. Dianne Cassere, "Diamonds Are Polished—So Is Nadine" (interview), in *Conversations*, p. 57.

16. Clingman, *Novels of Nadine Gordimer*, p. 30.

17. Bragg, "Solitude of a White Writer" (interview), p. 75.

18. Gordimer and Goldblatt, *Lifetimes*, p. 94.

19. Clingman, *Novels of Nadine Gordimer*, p. 64.

20. Ibid., p. 68.

21. Stephen Gray, "An Interview with Nadine Gordimer," in *Conversations*, p. 181.

CHAPTER THREE: KNOWING THROUGH THE BODY

1. Teichgraeber, "Cry for the Beloved Country" (interview), p. 26.

2. Diane Johnson, "Living Legends," review of *A Sport of Nature, New York Review of Books*, 16 July 1987.

3. Judith Thurman, "Choosing a Place," review of *A Sport of Nature, New Yorker*, 29 June 1987, p. 87.

4. Hurwitt, "The Art of Fiction," (interview), p. 131.

5. Teichgraeber, "Cry for the Beloved Country," (interview), p. 26.

6. Roland Barthes, *Writing Degree Zero*, quoted in Gordimer, "The Essential Gesture," p. 286.

7. Gordimer, "A Vision of Two Blood-Red Suns," in *The Essential Gesture*, p. 232.

8. Gordimer, "Pula!" in *The Essential Gesture*, p. 210.

9. Ibid., pp. 209–10.

10. Lipman, "Nadine Gordimer" (interview), pp. 108–9.

11. Nadine Gordimer, "A Style of Her Own," in *Friday's Footprint and Other Stories* (New York: Viking, 1960), pp. 78–79.

12. Gordimer, "A Brilliant Bigot," review of *Sarah Gertrude Millin, Times Literary Supplement*, 15 September 1978.

13. See also Newman, *Nadine Gordimer*, pp. 30–31.

14. Lipman, "Nadine Gordimer" (interview), p. 109.

15. Gordimer, "A Brilliant Bigot," *Times Literary Supplement*, 15 September 1978.

16. Junction Avenue Theatre Company, "Nadine Gordimer" (interview), p. 250.

17. Gordimer, "The Essential Gesture," *The Essential Gesture*, p. 298.

18. Thurman, "Choosing a Place," p. 90. Subsequent quotations are from pp. 88 and 87, respectively.

19. *New York Review of Books*, 16 July 1987, p. 9.

20. Thurman (review), *New Yorker*, p. 89.

21. Johnson, "Living Legends," p. 9.

22. Tom Wilhelmus, "Nothing Pretentious about Life and Art," *Hudson Review* 40 (1988): 669–71.

23. Thurman, "Choosing a Place," p. 88; Johnson, "Living Legends," p. 9.

24. Johnson, "Living Legends," p. 8.

25. Gordimer, "The Essential Gesture," p. 296.

26. Thurman, "Choosing a Place," p. 90.

27. *Women's Review of Books* IX, Dec., 1991, p. 8.

28. Sternhell, "Nadine Gordimer" (interview), p. 32.

29. Gordimer, "Living in the Interregnum," p. 280.

30. Gray, "Interview with Nadine Gordimer," p. 178.

31. Gordimer, "Living in the Interregnum," p. 281.

32. Gray, "Interview with Nadine Gordimer," p. 184.

CHAPTER FOUR: "WEBS OF FALSEHOOD"

1. Martin Luther King, Jr., "Letter from Birmingham Jail," *Why We Can't Wait;* quoted by Stephen B. Oates, *Let the Trumpet Sound* (New York: Harper and Row, 1982), p. 223.

2. See, for instance, the 1979 interview with Claude Servan-Schreiber, "Nadine Gordimer: A White African Against Apartheid," in *Conversations,* pp. 117–18.

3. Terry Gross, "Fresh Air: Nadine Gordimer" (interview), in *Conversations,* p. 310.

4. Similarly, "it seems to me that the two greatest drives in people's lives, the two most important things, are sex and politics." Fullerton-Smith, "Off the Page" (interview), *Conversations,* p. 299.

5. Cf. Newman, "The sexual double-entendre ('you satisfy') counters the threat by associating Maureen, July's economic 'mistress' in town, with his 'town woman'" (*Nadine Gordimer,* p. 90).

6. Clingman, *Novels of Nadine Gordimer,* p. 197, observes that Gina becomes fast friends with a black playmate, learning the language and customs of behavior from her; meanwhile, Victor adopts a submissive role in regard to July.

7. Adrienne Rich, "Natural Resources," in *The Dream of a Common Language* (New York: Norton, 1978), p. 67.

8. Clingman, *Novels of Nadine Gordimer,* p. 197.

9. Clingman's insight (*The Novels of Nadine Gordimer,* p. 202) is that this novel sees "the present through the eyes of the future . . . decoding the signs and codes of the present in the light of their actual reality."

10. The quoted phrase from Gramsci is the epigraph for *July's People.*

11. Gray, "Interview with Nadine Gordimer," p. 178.

12. I regret that Clingman's essay, "Writing out There," *English Academy Review* 3 (1985): 191–201, came to my attention too late to further this discussion.

13. Gordimer, "Censors and Unconfessed History," in *The Essential Gesture,* p. 259.

14. Lipman, "Nadine Gordimer" (interview), p. 111.

15. Ibid.

16. Teichgraeber, "Cry for the Beloved Country" (interview), p. 30.

17. Gray, "Interview with Nadine Gordimer," pp. 178–79.

CHAPTER FIVE: NO ONE KNOWS

1. Gray, "Interview with Nadine Gordimer," p. 178.

2. Christa Wolf, *Patterns of Childhood* (New York: Farrar, Straus and Giroux, 1984), p. 406.

3. Nadine Gordimer, *Six Feet of the Country* (New York: Simon & Schuster, 1956), pp. 87–97.

4. Ibid., p. 28.

5. Ibid., p. 38.

CHAPTER SIX: WHERE ONE MAKES A LIFE

1. Cooke, *Novels of Nadine Gordimer,* chapter two, rather misleadingly terms this motif "Leaving the Mother's House."

2. Compare Clingman, p. 31, on the limited role of blacks in the novel.

3. Newman, *Nadine Gordimer,* pp. 26–29, offers interesting commentary on the familial psychosexual motifs in the novel.

4. Gordimer, *Six Feet of the Country*, p. 114.

5. Gordimer, "From the Nobel Lecture," p. 24.

6. Babylonian Talmud, *Pirke Avot*, I, 14; the final quotations are from the Babylonian Talmud, *Sab.*, 31a, and *Pirke Avot*, II, 6, respectively.

INDEX